A Gift for:

From:

D0167254

Opening to God's Messages

An Invitation to Personal Reflection

To Emily,
May God's peace be with you -
Tammy Koenecke

Tammy Koenecke, RN, BSN, MASL

This book is dedicated to . . .

☙

*The Messenger, My God, The God of all Creation
and to . . .*

☙

*my loving husband, Keith, an unfailing source
of support, my soul mate,*

☙

*our wonderful sons and their amazing families,
true blessings in my life,*

☙

*my extended family that never lets me forget the
true meaning of family,*

☙

*. . . in an effort to share my faith with him/them in a
way that will live on long after my purpose here
on earth has been fulfilled.*

Table of Contents

Introduction   xi

CHAPTER 1—GOD'S CREATION   1

Give God the Credit   3
Summer Lights   6
The Smudge   9
A Message in the Flowers   12
The Palm of His Hand   15
In Due Time   18

CHAPTER 2—NURTURING YOUR SPIRIT   21

Having an "Ah" Moment   22
Knowing When to Stop   25
Let's Be Silly   28
Confidentiality or Mutual Respect   31
Be Yourself   34
Gratitude in All Things   37
A Blanket of Warmth   41

CHAPTER 3—FACING OUR FEARS   45

Listening For the Echo   46
Embracing the Struggle   49

False Evidence Appearing Real 52
It's Not _ _ _ _, Is It? 55
Weathering the Storm 58
Procrastination 62

CHAPTER 4—RELEASING CONTROL 65

Think For Yourself 67
Set a Goal 70
What to do With the Silence 73
The Author and The Storyteller 76
Deep Cleaning 79
I Should Know Better 81
Excuses, Excuses 84
The Other Side of the Bed 87
Begin Again 90

CHAPTER 5—HOPE AND TRUST 93

Just Wait 94
I Told You So 98
The Right Road 101
Spinning Out of Control 104
What's Good About It 107
The Correctly Arranged Path 110

CHAPTER 6—MAKING CONNECTIONS 113

Personal Connections 114
Message Worth Repeating 117
Cut the Chatter 121
It's Not About the Food 124
Step One 127
Hospitality 129

What Does It Mean   132
Have You Met My Spirit   135
A Woven World   138
Go Ahead, Say It   141
Touches of Life   144
Something is Missing   147

CHAPTER 7—CHANGE   151

Drop the Rock   152
Breaking the Cycle   155
Called to Grow   158
The Watchful Eye of God   161
Under Pressure   164
Daily Renewal   168
What's Next   171
Waves of Change   174

CHAPTER 8—ON THE ROAD   177

Lessons From a Scrabble Board   179
The Tie That Binds   182
Look Back   185
In the Midst of Chaos   188
A Room With a View   191
& Beyond   194

CHAPTER 9—READINESS   197

Message to Get Ready   198
The Final Chapter   201
Focus   204
What's the Secret   207
Trapped Inside   210
Time is Running Out   213

CHAPTER 10—REFLECTIONS FROM THE CHRISTMAS
AND NEW YEAR'S SEASON   217

It's the Most Wonderful Time of the Year?   218
Give Him a Room   221
In The Darkness of Night   224
Be the Light   227
Heart Gifts   230
You Will Grow Into It   233
A Season of Reflection   236
Pay Attention   239
Making Ends Meet   243
Incentives   246

Introduction

Well the time has come. What a joy this process has been. Over the past 10 plus years my work as a Registered Nurse in the area of Spiritual Care has allowed me to grow spiritually through writing personal reflections and sharing them with members of my community. A few years ago I was asked to create a book containing a collection of my personal reflections and here it is.

Totally unaware of the impact these reflections would have on my life I simply began to put on paper what I felt I was being called to share in regard to the connections between spirituality and health. I continue to believe that in order to be healthy as a whole person it is important to care for each part of the whole. Caring for the body, mind and spirit ensures that the whole person maintains optimal health. In addition, health does not always mean being free from illness or disease, but rather it is being comfortable, accepting, and grateful for what is ours. Deepening our spiritual health makes healing possible in the absence of curing. Many of the messages I received addressed these very issues.

The gift that has come to me from these messages, these promptings has been a blessing in my life. By taking the time to write down the messages God sent me I have been given the gift of a deeper relationship, a stronger connection to The Messenger, My God, The God of all Creation. You see I maintain that each of these messages have come to me from God through everyday life experiences, through nature, and through other people in a way that moved me to put them on paper for others to read and consider the personal application it might have for them. I usually type as fast as I can so as not to miss the message being sent. Then when I am finished I read the reflection grateful for the way it impacts my life personally. He sends the message; I simply type it onto the paper. I become a vessel for his message to be delivered.

You may find that some of the messages have been left in present tense as I usually wrote them and sent them out monthly. Many I have adjusted as they continue to apply in the here and now. You may also find grammatical errors and it will be my request that you overlook them to see the meaning rather than the structure.

It is my hope that you will enjoy this collection and be Open to God's Messages as they apply to your life. Trusting that after reading them you, too, will have a deeper relationship with The Messenger, Your God, The God of all Creation.

CHAPTER I

God's Creation

The Message

I sent a message to you today
Did you get it I sent it right away
I didn't Lord, it was a crazy day
but anyway what did it say
I sent it in the early light
as you woke from the dark of night
It said, "I'm here for you again today,
you need only call, I'm here to stay

I sent another, I tried again
to contact you my dear friend

I didn't Lord, it was a crazy day
but anyway what did it say
With the brightest light and warmest sun
full aware that you were on the run
I sent it at noon sure to reach you then
to say, "I am listening for you my friend"

I tried again at evening light
this time you had to get it, right
I didn't Lord, it was a crazy day
but anyway what did it say
I thought surely that the evening sky
would be the ticket to catch your eye
It said "I have not left you, nor will I leave
you need only to believe"

Give God the Credit

৵৶

The next time you hear a baby laugh or see an ocean wave, take note. Pause and listen as His Majesty whispers ever so gently, "I'm here." —MAX LUCADO

৵৶

Spring is a wonderful time of year. The birds have returned and are singing in the early morning hours. Flowers and tender grass shoots are sprouting through the dark earth. The smell of spring captures my attention as I walk out the door. All around are signs of God's presence through his creation, signs of hope in dark times. I want to share with you a little insight on our need to give credit where credit is due.

Our grandchildren were staying with us one weekend, Braeden was 3 and his brother Rylan was 2. One night we were driving home and there was just a sliver of moon in the sky. The light from that sliver illuminated the entire circumference of the moon. My eyes were drawn to look beyond the sliver, to all there was beyond the sliver. I quietly thanked God for his presence in our lives. I pointed it out the boys. They were delighted to see the moon and Braeden announced, "Gama, God put the moon in the sky". I agreed with him and then his little brother, Rylan, chimed in, "Hey, Papa, I put the moon in the sky". My husband, Keith, and I chuckled. It is just so fun when kids start to talk and Rylan enjoyed parroting his brother.

When we got home we purposefully walked outside to see the moon one more time. Rylan pointed at the moon and said, "Look, Papa, I put the moon in the sky". Braeden wanting to counsel his little brother walked over to him, put his hand on his shoulder and looked him in the eyes and said, "No Rylan, God put the moon in the sky!" As he walked toward the house, Rylan followed his brother with his head down slightly and softly said, "I put the moon in the sky." It was all I could do to keep a straight face. This interaction was so precious.

Maybe sometimes we forget who put the moon in the sky. I think sometimes we take for granted the coming of spring. We hurry it along. We question why it is taking so long to come. We criticize the length of winter as if we are trying to manage it, as if we can orchestrate it. Then when spring does arrive we say things like, "it is about time", "I can't believe it took so long", as if we have control over God's creation. I wonder if we take the time to give credit where credit is due. Do we stand in awe of the creator for the things he has done that we as humans cannot do?

Beyond this question, do we look at the night sky as though it is just part of our life or do we look beyond the sliver of light, the glimmer of hope, toward the open arms of God? Deep within us is a seed of hope, a springtime of our life waiting to burst forth. God is working to bring that hope to fullness of life and like the sliver of moon that cast a light bright enough to illuminate the circumference of the moon he sends us glimmers of hope as well. Through gentle sprouts of new life, morning bird songs, and earthy fragrance we know that God is working, always working to create something good. There are moments in our life when God sends us glimmers of hope, promising to work all things for the good. A phone call that keeps us from overdoing, a stranger that comes along just in time to help us. These are not things that we as humans do. These are things God does to remind us of his constant presence.

At a young age these 2 little boys were aware or rather were becoming aware of the fact that there are things we as humans cannot do. There are some things only God can do. We cannot put the moon in the sky and although I can plant flowers in the fall, I cannot bring them to life in the spring. Someone greater does that for me-*and for you.* May we always praise God for the newness of life and in all things *Give God the Credit.*

Questions to ponder:
When was the last time I gave God credit for
the way things worked out?
Do I try to control the uncontrollable?

Summer Lights

❧❧

*The heavens tell of the glory of God. The skies display his
marvelous craftsmanship. Day after day they continue
to speak; night after night they make him known. They
speak without a sound or a word; their voice is silent in
the skies; yet their message has gone out to all the earth,
and their words to all the world. —PSALM 19:1-4*

❧❧

Have you ever enjoyed something so much that you could not
wait to tell someone about it? Have you ever wanted to share
an experience it in such a way that it would inspire someone to
want to experience it themselves? Well, I want to share a story
with you that continues to make my spirit smile. The topic of
this reflection simply has to be summer lights.

I often hear people talk about the beautiful summer nights,
but not so often do I hear about the beauty of the summer lights.
One Friday night in July my husband and I took the opportunity to spend an evening out on a piece of land we own in the
country, quite a distance from towns or villages where the street
lights can distort the natural lighting of the night sky, our purpose; to watch the stars come out. I had campaigned for this
venture for a couple of years and finally we were off to do some
star gazing, little did I know we were in for a show.

Having waited so long for this evening to come for us to
simply experience the summer sky I became nervous when the
clouds started moving in about 8:00 p.m. My anticipated sky
watching was being threatened by cloud cover. I quietly prayed
for God to push away the clouds so that I could see the first star
of evening pierce the dark sky.

As we walked across the acreage darkness began to slip between the daisies, bee balm, and tall blades of grass. The show was about to start. My eyes began to adjust to the darkness and then about 9:00 p.m. the clouds began to break up and we settled into a spot for watching the night sky. I anxiously awaited the first light in the darkness. What a surprise when the first summer light in the night was that of a firefly flickering allusively across the horizon against the tall grass; first one, then two, then ten, then twenty. They twinkled in front of us as if they were the opening act. My spirit began to giggle.

Not to be outdone the first star in the sky appeared in the blink of an eye. It did not start out as a dim light gaining power over time. No, it popped into place bright and beautiful. Methodically, one by one other stars popped into place until as if on cue hundreds at a time sparkled in the sky. What a show. We had started counting the stars and within minutes there was no possible way to count the stars. Meanwhile the fireflies kept up their end of the show, flashing in front of us vying for attention. My spirit laughed out loud.

We began to notice flashes of light coming from behind us, but bright enough to flash in front of us. We were not sure if the flashes were fireworks or what exactly. With some attention to the direction of the flashes we determined it was lightning. Around the edges of a clear sky flashes like those from a camera lit up the night. We crawled into the truck as the lightning took on a much more distinct form, that of a lightning bolt! What a show! My spirit was exhilarated.

It was about 10:30 when the rain came and the lightning danced around the sky with sharp bolts and soft flashes causing the raindrops to sparkle on the windows of the truck. We settled in, the rain doing its part in lulling us to sleep. Sometime later I woke for the final act in summer lights. There straight up in the sky was an amazing gentle moon with a glow that cast light across the valleys and into the window of the truck nudging me to pay attention. And I did. I watched as the wet foliage glistened in the moonlight. My spirit was in reverent awe.

So many things in life are taken for granted. The amazing summer lights are a gift from God. The show did not cost us one penny, but the impact on my spirit was priceless. Those of you who have read my reflections before know that the sky is my communication tool with God. I believe he had a message for me that evening in the summer lights. Some summer night find a back road in the country, or a piece of land (with permission) and stay late into the night watching the summer lights. I can assure you if you watch with your spirit you will not be disappointed. You will be enlightened!

Questions to ponder:
Where do I find God's messages waiting for me?
What makes my spirit giggle?

The Smudge

❧❧

Lord, remind me how brief my time on earth will be.
Remind me that my days are numbered, and that
my life is fleeing away.
My life is no longer than the width of my hand.
An entire lifetime is just a moment to you; human
existence is but a breath.
We are merely moving shadows, and all our busy
rushing ends in nothing.
We heap up wealth for someone else to spend.
And so, Lord, where do I put my hope?
My only hope is in you. —PSALM 39:4-7

❧❧

The sky offers me messages from God and many times they are simply messages of his unfailing love and constant presence in my life. However, when I get the same message more than once I am led to reflect on the message more deeply. Recently, a message came to me in the evening sky. It was a smudge. The horizon was filled with white, billowy, cotton. Each cloud had clearly defined edges against the blue sky. There were definite rays of soft pink and yellow reaching out from behind the clouds and I smiled to myself as I marveled at the beauty. Then as my eyes grazed across the sky there was this smudge! Let's reflect on the smudge.

Where did this come from? How did it get into this perfect picture? Why was it there interrupting the beautiful definition and clarity of the evening sky? As strange as it was to be there in my vision, I was drawn to examine the smudge. Have you ever painted something and before it was dry brushed up against it or polished a glass or piece of fine jewelry and then touched it with your finger. A smudge forms and for me disappointment follows. The hard work seems to be all for naught. I sometimes question whether it is worth the work to make things nice when they just seem to get smudged anyway!

Well the smudge in the sky was similar to this kind of experience. It was a disappointment to me, at first. Why in this beautiful display of clouds would there be a smudge? What was God thinking? Perhaps God brushed up against it accidentally. He does paint the sky after all! It certainly was a curiosity to me, but I forgot about it or so I thought. A few nights later the smudge appeared again. Not an accident I said to myself, there is something more here in this message from the sky. I cannot remember ever noticing a smudge like this before. Yes indeed there had to be a message for me to share from this smudge in the sky. So, I have been thinking about it ever since. What meaning did it have for you and me? And once again God revealed his deeper message to me and the answer came as follows.

Could it be the smudge represents those times in our lives when things are unclear to us, when there is no clarity in our life purpose or the times in our lives when we are disappointed? Throughout our lives we have experiences for which we have many questions and no answers. We can be sailing along just fine and be struck with an illness, loss or pain that puts a smudge on our life picture with no answers to the why questions. We may seem to be the picture of health physically and have some disease intruding our body with no answers to the why questions. We may seem happy on the outside but be crying on the inside with no answers to the why questions. Life may lose its clearly defined edges and become smudged.

As I pondered this smudge in the sky and looked more closely at it I discovered three things; first; there was added depth to the sky by its presence, second; there was clarity and confusion in the same space and third; the unblemished sky still existed behind the smudge.

Isn't life like that? We are encouraged to search and look deeper into the meaning of our life when we are faced with adversity. We gain depth of compassion for others through our own adversity.

Clarity and confusion will always be a part of this life. Although, we generally enter our daily routines anticipating the same outcome from our actions, we are not exempt from changes, which cause us to be disillusioned. We find ourselves in a state of confusion. We long for things to become clear to us. We want answers when there are none. Confusion covers our hope like the smudge in the sky.

We must remember that hope is always there behind the smudge on our clear picture of life. The glass remains perfect behind the fingerprint. In time the smudge is removed and beauty restored, but not without leaving resiliency. Did you know that fine china is actually strengthened by our touch? The oils of our hands somehow strengthen the china. Yes, the smudges make us stronger, too. We become more resilient. The smudge over time is removed and our hope restored. We hold on to the hope behind the confusion knowing full well that hope exists the same as the clear billowy clouds behind the smudge in sky.

The beauty of life is made more real when we encounter confusion. There is a new appreciation for simple things. We begin to understand the troubles of another person as we encounter trouble ourselves. Adversity adds depth to our lives and the confusion helps us to see more clearly the hope, which remains constant. The smudge in the sky was not just a mistake in God's painting those nights but an opportunity for me to take in the beauty of that which was clear to me and trust that God knows what he is doing in the smudge.

Questions to ponder:
What have been the smudges in my life?
What did I gain from them?

A Message in the Flowers

⁂

But those who wait on the Lord will find new strength.
They will fly high on wings like eagles. They will run and
not grow weary. They will walk and not faint.
—ISAIAH 40:31

⁂

The flowers have been gorgeous this summer and filled with messages for me as a rooky gardener. You see I trust God to take care of the gardening he always does a fabulous job, I pluck weeds and move plants occasionally but God usually uses the wind to move plants in my garden. The wind can also be damaging. Let me tell you a story about the wind, my flower garden and the message that lies within.

Early this summer the wind had been very forceful in a storm and my daisies which had been dancing in the breezes days before were suddenly lying on the ground. It had been a busy weekend so I quickly entered the garden and scooped up the weakened stems in an effort to set them upright. It seemed as though they were destined to die, so weak and down trodden. I left the garden with sadness in my heart for their short lives. I vowed that I would at least save them for flower vases and enjoy them inside for a few more days.

Three days passed before I remembered that I needed to salvage the daisies for my kitchen table. As I set out for my early morning walk I glanced at the garden and vowed I would enter again and cut the blooms that had been knocked to the ground with the wind. As I entered the garden I was struck by what awaited my entering. The blooms I was certain would be withering by now were full of color and strength. I crouched down to look more closely as I was amazed. Touching the stems I began to separate them for cutting and found that many of them had worked their way into an upright position once again. Several of them had severe 90 degree turns in their stalks. Some had circular stems. Many stalks careened around the heaviness of the others which had fallen on them.

There was a beautiful message in this discovery for me. These flowers were not giving up on God to take care of them. They were determined to change their direction, reconfigure themselves in such a way that they would be able to receive the necessary light to survive. Isn't this a terrific message for each of us? As we are burdened with heaviness, broken by tragedy, downtrodden with sadness or pain, we too can change our sense of direction, stretch our boundaries and turn toward God who waits patiently while we determine which way to go. God never deserts us. He never looses his faith in us as his children to seek his support.

Doesn't it seem as though it is in times of trouble, despair and anguish that we turn our hearts toward the son. The Son of God. We ask Jesus to help us in our pain and suffering. We gain the strength we need to move forward, to overcome the pressures placed on us. And we often do it more easily in a group. When we have others who are experiencing a similar situation we pull together and support one another. Then with each accomplishment of a member of the group we are encouraged and strive to become even stronger.

The flowers did this. I could see the way they had grown together each in a different direction yet each striving for the same goal, nourishment from their creator. We are called to be encouragers of one another. Each of us has within us the ability to overcome great obstacles because the Holy Spirit lives within us, but the process is accelerated when we are supported by others around us. Our faith families provide us with support. Our relatives and friends offer us an opportunity to tap into wisdom regarding coping skills. We are one in Christ. Each of us is expected to offer a hand, a smile, a hug, a kind word, to those in need of lifting up.

When stormy winds blow through our lives and cause us to be knocked down we must retain the hope and promise of God that he will not leave us or abandon us, that he will walk through the valley of death with us, that he will lift us up on eagles wings. God sends his reminders of his love for us all the time through his glorious creation. Be aware of your surroundings for God is speaking to you. Our great source of strength is waiting for us to turn our lives toward the Son.

Questions to ponder:
How does my garden grow?
What can I learn from it?

The Palm of His Hand

ॐॐ

*To see the world in a grain of sand and a heaven in a
wildflower: Hold infinity in the palm of your hand,
and eternity in an hour.* —WILLIAM BLAKE

ॐॐ

As I walked through the woods one day in May I reflected upon this question; what does it mean to be held in the palm of his hand? Pondering this question I discovered new insight into the beauty of my own hand and the enormity of His hands. Let me explain.

As I walked I paid particular attention to the work of God's hands beneath my feet and above my head. Two views were especially stimulating for my reflection. The first was an area on the hillside deep within the woods where light entered through the canopy between the branches and newly formed leaves. The floor of the woods was covered with dead oak leaves, yet new life peaked between the leaves. Signs of hope forged forth with delicate stems and pastel colors. There in this 10 foot square of dead oak leaves were scattered flowers. Some of the flowers were the size of my pinky fingernail. As if painted on, the delicate petals wore varying shades of pink. Next to them circles of purple with white centers stood steadily on the hillside. Ovals of vivid yellow and spots of bright white covered the area, each flower pushing past the evidence of loss in the dead oak leaves. God's hands had made these flowers, placed them there as a reminder to me of the new life he offers each of us.

Not far from these tiny messengers stood two trees to which my eyes were drawn. There they stood solid next to one another. As my eyes moved up the trunks toward the foliage at the top there was an amazing sight. About 25 feet up a branch from one tree had extended toward the other and it was totally wrapped in this second tree. It was as if the branch extended for support and this tree embraced it lovingly. From that point the two trees continued skyward about 10 feet before any other branches appeared.

It was windy and they swayed together supportive of one another. This symbolized for me the loving gentleness of God's hand as I reach out for support and he embraces my pain or struggle and sways with me as I work my way upward.

The earth is filled with representation of God's loving hands and as we awaken our senses to the unfolding messages around us we generate spiritual growth. If we are to ponder the question about what it means to be held in the palm of God's hand let's also consider the palms of our own hands. What does it mean for us to use our hands to provide for others? How do we show comfort, support, stability, and hope through our hands?

Hands of gentleness, caring, loving, compassion and strength are the busy hands of God. They know the difference between meaningful and meaningless work. They extend to feel the texture of God's handy-work. They are lifted in praise and thanksgiving for the expanse of the sky. They fold in prayer for those in need of support and healing. Our hands are an extension of God's hands. For me the earth and sky are the palms of God's hands and you and I are being held in the midst of them. We are being supported by them. My hands then and yours are extensions of God's hands toward others helping them to stand strong and reach skyward like the two trees. Our hands are the hands of hope that God offers in the delicate flowers on the wooded floor.

One of my favorite songs is, *On Eagles Wings*, based on Psalm 91, and in the refrain we sing, "And he will raise you up on eagle's wings, bear you on the breath of dawn, make you to shine like the sun and hold you in the palm of his hand". What does it mean for you to be held in the palm of His hand?

In a beautiful hand meditation, Father Edward Farrell writes after describing the act of holding someone else's hand, "Whose Hand was that? It could have been any hand. It could have been God's hand. It was! God has no other hands than ours." Our hands are indeed the physical hands of God.

Questions to ponder:
Do my hands embrace the world the way the work of God's hands embraces me?
How do I experience the palm of His hand?

In Due Time

... and provide for those who grieve in Zion—to bestow on them a crown of beauty instead of ashes, the oil of gladness instead of mourning, and a garment of praise instead of despair. They will be called oaks of righteousness, a planting of the Lord of rthe display of his splendor. —ISAIAH 61:3

What an amazing spring. It was hard for me to remember one like it. The color in the woods unfolded so slowly allowing me to take in the varying colors of new growth with deep and light shades of green. Reds and purples soon followed. The fragrance of spring filled my senses as I walked along the countryside, lilacs, apple blossoms, fresh cut grass and the smell of over turned soil, each fragrance mingling together to create the fragrance of spring. Then one day as I was driving admiring the process I noticed in the distance a mighty oak tree. It stood alone in the center of the freshly turned soil without a bud to be seen, as if announcing, I am taking my time, I will bloom and grow and meld with the rest soon enough, but for now I wait. I want to reflect on the things that come in due time.

Like the mighty oak that waits patiently for change to occur, not the least bit shaken by the fact that all the other trees around it seemed eager to display their foliage, we sometimes need that extra time to become comfortable with exposing our inner beauty regardless of what the rest of the world thinks. In grief we need to take the time we need to become comfortable returning to life. In the case of the oak tree, leaves of new life will present themselves in due time. New growth will become evident and the extra time will have helped to establish the stamina needed to support the new branches, the new branches that will serve as resting points for birds and small animals. I continued to watch the oak over the weeks of springtime as it allowed the last few leaves to be released and let go. I watched as the buds began to peek out and then slowly open into leaves, leaves that will become large and strong throughout the summer.

For those who grieve, the time needed to accept the changes in their life is as unique as they are. Each person requires their own amount of time. They cannot be rushed. They should not be rushed. I have seen individuals face changes in their lives that only they could achieve and they do. In due time. In their time. Not mine. Not the worlds. In their time. They come to a place where they can allow the buds of new life to be seen ever so slightly and then as if comforted by that first step reveal their inner beauty again to the world. Forever changed. Stronger. Broader. More open to the needs of others. They, too, allow their lives to be open like the branches on the giant oak for others to come and rest and be supported.

They are patient, courageous, and wise. They are examples for us to look to when we face challenging times in our own lives. I know it is not easy. Many have told me it is not easy. The hope they found to be patient, be courageous, came from deep within. God's presence within held them fast when they could not move. His presence helped them stand when they were sure their legs would give way. His presence was a sounding board for the emotions tumbling inside. I believe it is this inner hope that urges the buds of the mighty oak to take that step and peek forth, the inner hope that urges us to expose our inner beauty just a little at a time slowly working toward returning to full abundant life.

When change comes your way I hope you will think about the mighty oak standing alone in the plowed field patiently waiting for the inner strength it needs to push forth the buds of new life, all in due time.

Questions to ponder:
Have I felt impatient about a change in my life?
How do I regain direction?

CHAPTER 2

Nurturing the Spirit

Morning Prayer

*Good Morning Lord and this I pray
That you will be with me today,
Walk with me each passing minute
Help me to remain within it,
Not ahead and not behind
But in the present may I find,
A quiet peace and gentle love
From you Dear Father, up above*

Having an "Ah" Moment

೨೭

Deep within your very being is the driving force
of your life, your Spirit.
Nurture your spirit daily with activities that
bring you "Ah"

೨೭

One morning as I awoke there was a conflict in my being. My head knew I had to arise to meet the day and get to work, but my body ached to stay in bed. For me this conflict is always about my spirit. Wholeness requires health of body, mind and spirit. I felt disconnected and I was suddenly aware that it was my spirit that needed attention. I began with prayer for the energy I needed to get out of bed and tend to my spiritual need. I want to share with you what I learned by having an "Ah" moment.

Walking is such a powerful spiritual nurturing activity for me. So, I donned my walking shoes and out I went to experience the fullness of the outdoors. The smells of spring, the slight warmth of the southern breeze all contributed to my experience. Legs stretching out now my being began to settle and a feeling of "Ah" washed over me. This morning's activities are not all that different than many mornings, but today I was inclined to wonder about ways to describe the spiritual part of my wholeness. I wondered about a way to help you discover the spiritual part of your wholeness.

Well, many things as you can imagine began to come to mind. The spirit is the inner most part of your being, the driving force of your life, it is the divine within you. Though these statements seem obvious it is still perhaps hard to comprehend the spirit, something so intangible. We do not easily see the spirit within ourselves. Our physical being is much more easily described. Let's see female, 5 foot 2 inches tall, brown hair (you can add wild to that description on many days!), blue eyes, etc., etc. are words to describe my physical being. The mind can also be described with character traits. Some people are thinkers using their minds to solve challenging problems and some are feelers using their intuition, which leads them to reach out in areas of need. I tend to be more of a feeler than a thinker.

When I begin to put words to the description of my spirit, however, the keyboard is slow to respond. Luckily for me this morning I was given and "Ah" moment that was so profound I realized that God was sending me a way to describe the spirit within me and a way for you to discover the spirit within you. As I walked my spirit settled and I felt total peace. No more clamoring in my head about getting up and going this morning. No more aching in my muscles and joints urging me to stay in bed. I felt total peace. My spirit was being fed allowing my mind to slow down and my body to stop aching. I felt whole.

Now, I want you to think about times when you have had an "Ah" moment. Not an "Ah Ha" moment when you realize the answer to a difficult question or finally put two and two together figuring out how people are related. Not an "Oh" moment when you are surprised. Not a "Wow" that was wonderful or amazing moment, but an "Ah" moment. The kind of moment that brings you comfort, peace, tranquility, contentment. The kind of moment perhaps that you feel at the end of an exhilarating run, a bike ride, or a swim. The kind of moment that comes after quieting yourself for 5 minutes at the end of the day. The kind of moment that comes when you set yourself down into the most comfortable chair in the house.

You see it is not so much about what the spirit looks like, but rather what it is like. When you can realize you are having an "Ah" moment you are on the way to uncovering the spiritual dimension of your wholeness and discovering what makes your spirit healthy. You can use those activities to nurture your spirit.

There are many educational resources out there telling us how to keep our bodies healthy. Things like exercise, eating right, and reducing your exposure to toxins are all great ways to provide care to your body. Research demonstrates that our minds remain healthier if they are challenged with puzzles, reading, writing, even dancing. We can read about these tangible things to do to keep our bodies and our minds in tiptop shape and most of these suggestions are universal in producing healthy responses.

The spirit is a different matter. Not everyone's spirit feels nurtured by the suggestions in a book. You must first discover what makes your spirit go "Ah" then and only then will you be on the right track for providing nourishment to your spirit.

Pay attention to the times when your spirit elicits an "Ah". Make note of it. Use this activity to nurture your spirit regularly. If you do not experience an "Ah" moment then maybe your spirit has been neglected for so long it has given up trying to alert you to its needs. Pray for guidance, quiet yourself, be in nature and try to stir your spirit to its welcome position in your wholeness. It works for me.

Questions to ponder:
Where to I find my "Ah" moments?
How would I explain them to a friend?

Knowing When to Stop

ٷٷ

There is more to life than merely increasing its speed.
—*GANDHI*

ٷٷ

I love autumn, for a number of reasons. I love the colors. I love the fresh crisp air. I love the smell of the harvest. But one thing I especially love is nature's message to stop. Let this be the topic of reflection, knowing when to stop.

Every fall the trees and plants stop. They stop producing fruit. They dry down readying the crop for harvest. They lose their leaves, perhaps relieving the heavy burden of their weight and the constant pull of the wind on the branches. There is so much to be learned from this cycle of nature. The trees and plants are not afraid of what others will think if they stop. They instinctively know they will gain strength through this intended action of inaction.

Can we stop? Can you stop? Can I stop? What will happen if you or I stop for a period of time and take an intended action of inaction, if we release the burden of tasks weighing us down long enough to regain strength? After all, many people do depend on us for all sorts of things. Surely, we will be letting someone down? In reality, we are likely to benefit more from stopping to take a rest than we can ever know. So, how do we do it? Do we need to look for the right time? Will the right time ever come? Will we ever have enough money saved, recognition achieved, or problems solved to stop? In a book I read entitled, *Sabbath: Finding Rest, Renewal, and Delight In Our Busy Lives*, by Wayne Muller, I found this comment, "You cannot buy stop", and as I read that statement I paused to reflect on the deeper message here.

Stop is not an outcome to be achieved through hard work or monetary investments. It is an action to be taken. In our society we put a lot of stock in outcomes often considering only the immediate outcome. Therefore, if something stops we fear the immediate loss or anticipate that life will become bogged down, like those silly credit card commercials. How embarrassing it would be if you were the cause of a slowdown in the machine of progress, anyway the marketing folks want you to believe that people are watching your every move and if it interferes with the fast pace of the day then you will be frowned upon.

Is this the reason we hesitate to stop, rest, and retreat? Is it because of what others might say about us? Do we fear people will say, "What happened to so and so, they used to be so active?" or "They used to take phone calls after office hours". The gossip will flourish. Gossip is a spirit crusher and we often make our decisions based on the desire to not be the center of gossip. But the absence of rest is also a spirit crusher. We must make a choice and it should be with our own well-being in mind. Jesus modeled this action for us. We read in Luke 5:15-16, "Yet despite Jesus' instruction, the report of his power spread even faster, and vast crowds came to hear him preach and to be healed of their diseases. But Jesus often withdrew to the wilderness for prayer". Jesus understood the importance of stopping from time to time to care for himself, to listen to the Father.

You and I need to identify the long-term personal benefits of stopping, resting, retreating. More than likely they will have a positive effect on you, one which will add strength and vitality to your spirit, offer an acquisition of wisdom, or deepen your sense of belonging to the bigger picture of creation. God has created a natural cycle for all things to stop, rest, listen, and start anew.

The colors of fall remind us that we, being part of God's creation, need to stop, rest, listen and start anew.

We cannot buy stop. It is not something to be achieved through hard work or monetary investment. It is not something we acquire through others. So let go of the idea that you are the only one who can complete the task. Listen to your spirit calling you to stop and rest and trust God to provide in your absence.

Questions to ponder:
Is it time for me to stop? Rest? Retreat?
Who will support me in your efforts to take care of myself?

Let's Be Silly

ꙮ

*A cheerful heart is good medicine, but a broken spirit
saps a person's strength.*
—PROVERBS 17:22 (NLT)

ꙮ

During the winter months of 2010 I had several opportunities to spend time with our grandchildren who ranged in age from 20 months to 3 years. Those times were just a hoot. Children offer us a perspective on life that often gets covered up in our efforts to be productive. I noticed that when I would tell one of them that they were being silly, they would light up, laugh and say, "watch this", trying to outdo their first antic. Pretty soon the room would be filled with laughter and silliness. Silly is a good thing to children, so when did silly become a bad thing for adults? I want to reflect with you on ways we can adopt silliness for a positive effect on our spirit.

Let me start by defining the word silly. If you looked in a dictionary you may find the definition of silly to be foolishness or frivolous and upon further investigation into the definition of these words come to the conclusion that silly refers to someone who does not have any common sense, or means to act irresponsibly, or to lack a sense of seriousness about a circumstance. In those terms I guess we might view silly as bad. However, the silly I am referring to is the ability to be light hearted about life, the ability to laugh and the ability to make others laugh even in difficult times.

Somewhere in my growing older I have lost the ability to do silly things without feeling embarrassed. I should act my age you know! What does that mean anyway? Is there a book out there somewhere that outlines activities allowed per age group? When I think about it, saying 'that is silly' to a 2 or 3 year old produces laughter, but somehow along the way the words change to 'don't be silly', which produce emotions of embarrassment, shame or guilt.

Sometimes as adults we begin to take every aspect of our life seriously and I believe that adds stress to our lives. Perhaps if we were to add one silly act per day (or start with one per week) to our lives we would reduce our stress level and boost the health of our spirit. Think about the possibilities for improved health, better relationships and positive attitudes. This might be a good research project for some budding student! Well, I have come to realize that for me life is too short to eliminate silliness entirely and I am determined to reintroduce a little silliness into my life.

I have begun asking myself these questions at the end of the day; have I done anything silly today, how did it make me feel and did I make anyone laugh today? I ask my husband the same questions. I am also trying to incorporate some silly things we can do together. One day we went walking in the rain without an umbrella, actually, it was still wintery and although that might seem irresponsible it made us laugh. It was silly. We laughed at ourselves for purposely leaving the umbrella behind and heading out into the cold wet weather, flinching at the cold raindrops on our faces, picking up the pace as if we could get away from them. I am sure there is a mother reading this thinking *pneumonia!* We did not catch pneumonia although I will not deny that the thought did go through my mind while we were walking!

You see I think there are opportunities for us to do little things that are silly in ways that will not harm our financial situation, our health, or our families and friends. Simple little things like skipping up the driveway after getting the mail (which is also good exercise), setting the table backwards, putting a funny picture in a frame for the world to see or millions of other ideas can produce laughter and lift the spirit after a long hard burden-some day.

There is tragedy all around us, worldwide and locally. There is great reason for concern about the future, our health, our economy, our food resources, and on and on. Without any way to release some of the stress we harbor our spirit can become smothered. I encourage you to remove a layer of that heavy coat of sensibility, do something silly, and allow yourself to laugh at yourself. If you are lucky you will make someone else laugh and lift their spirit, too.

Questions to ponder:
When was the last time I did something silly?
How did it make me feel?
Have I told the story to someone else to lift their spirits?

Confidentiality or Mutual Respect

ೲ

*When you respect another person you honor their need
for confidentiality and build trust into your relationships.*

ೲ

Each spring new growth earns our respect as we watch it push forth from the depths of the earth. As I watch it unfold, I wonder what the world would be like if we offered each other the same kind of respect we give the gentle buds of springtime. I want to share with you some of my observations about the concepts of confidentiality and mutual respect.

We hear so much about confidentiality. Everything in our personal lives is to be kept confidential. Organizations from hospitals to electric companies provide us with information about our rights and their commitment to ensuring that information will be kept confidential. Organizations have been mandated to establish standards for maintaining confidentiality. Have we gone too far? Have we lost sight of what could be a simpler approach to dealing with one another?

If we were to live by the words found in Romans 12:10, "Love each other with genuine affection, and take delight in honoring each other", I believe there would be no need to scurry around creating policies and getting signatures from people. Do we really have to get signatures to ensure that people have been given information about their rights to privacy? Isn't providing respect for one another a more genuine way of offering them privacy?

Definitions of respect include, "to esteem, to consider, consideration". Would this be ultimately what the whole confidentiality issue is about? Has there been a lack of consideration of others within our society that has lead us to require written proof of being considerate of one another? Interestingly honor is also defined as "great respect". To live our lives honoring others would meet the need I believe we are trying to accomplish in a more complete way.

What we really should do with the confidentiality issue is provide respect for privacy and individuals needs. Interestingly confidentiality means, "to keep secret". I find there are no secrets in this world. In fact, when things are suppose to be kept a secret they are more likely to be disclosed aren't they? Think of the little child who is asked to keep a secret about a parent's birthday gift. I have heard a child say, "Daddy, mommy got you golf clubs and it's a secret". I do not mean to say that organizations that have standards for confidentiality are merely keeping secrets. That is not it at all. I simply want to help you to reflect on the much deeper process for meeting this intention of maintaining confidentiality by becoming respectful of others and by honoring others.

As I travel around the community, county and state I love to take the time to watch people and their interaction with others. I love to look into their eyes and imagine the Holy Spirit alive in them. If we automatically assume respect for the Holy Spirit then their spirit is valuable and deserves honor and respect. I cannot imagine looking at someone and judging him or her to not be worthy of respect. I am not to judge. We are not to judge. If we keep this concept clear in our mind it becomes easier to respect and honor others.

In regard to the movement across this country to standardize confidentiality I worry about the actual and potential problems arising. God has asked us to carry one another's burdens. In Galatians 6:2 we read, "Share each other's troubles and problems, and in this way obey the law of Christ". Herein lies the conflict. If no one is to know about our troubles or problems, no one will be there to support us through our troubles or problems. There seems to be a fine line between confidentiality and support. If, however, we could trust that our troubles and problems would be viewed with respect and honor for what we are experiencing we would be open to sharing information.

I would also venture to say that no matter how confidentially my history is kept, if anyone wanted to know anything about me they would find it out in less time than it is taking you to read this letter. I continue to get junk mail; my home address can be located on map quest within seconds. If I believe that my life is private I am only kidding myself. I would rather strive for respect, consideration from others that my life is my own experience and not to be judged by anyone but God. I also pray that others will support my troubles and problems in this world.

Currently, buzzwords like confidentiality, rights, and privacy fill the literature. I hope to see the day when God's words of honor and respect become buzzwords for our society. No more secrets only genuine support for one another through honor and respect.

Questions to ponder:
What is my experience with confidentiality?
How do I show honor and respect to others?
Which would I rather have confidentiality or mutual respect? Why?

Be Yourself

≈

Happiness is the sense that one matters.
SAMUEL SHOEMAKER

≈

The winter winds can be very strong. I found a message in them one day as I was walking. If you are walking against a driving wind you have to exert extra effort to stay the course. When you walk with the wind you find your task much easier. I found a similarity in the desire for people to be themselves. It is easier to go with the flow than to stand-alone against the crowd and be yourself. I would like to encourage each of you to be yourself and for many of you that might start with the question, Who Am I?

Sometimes we live our lives for others. We find ourselves doing what we think others expect us to do. Often well meaning parents, siblings, spouses and even children offer advice in such a way that we may feel guilty if we do not take their advice. Perhaps we have even encouraged our loved ones to take paths that are actually our own unfulfilled dreams.

As parents, grandparents, mentors, friends, we need to avoid the temptation to live our dreams through the children. We must resist blocking their goals and dreams. We must not stand in the way of their moves. I am not suggesting we let children do whatever they want. Certainly, we have a responsibility as parents/adults to guide children safely through life. What I am trying to say here is that we need to nurture the development of their unique personality. We can begin by nurturing and respecting our own unique personality.

Have you ever set a goal in your mind without following through with the details to see the goal to completion? We become fearful of failure or of what others might think. We may feel as though we are too old or that we do not have the funds to pursue our dreams. We may feel as though we are too busy. Believe me I know a number of excuses. I have heard many and have used a few myself over the years.

Over the past years, I have been enlightened to the fact that if I am meant to do something or become someone I will be lead in the right direction if I seek divine guidance. It is my belief that God has a purpose for each of us and we travel through life uncovering our unique purpose. Years ago at a conference held at the Franciscan Spirituality Center in La Crosse, WI, I was prompted to think more deeply about whom I am and what keeps me from allowing myself to be, simply be me. I have forgotten the exact details of the story, but I strongly remember the theme. The story was about a man of great wisdom who was dying. A gentleman asked him to share some last words of wisdom for living life more fully. The dying man told him, "When you meet the Lord the Lord will not ask you, why were you not like your brother, your father, your friend. God will ask, why were you not yourself". In other words, God will not ask me why I was not Sara, Tiffany, Martha or Mary. He will only be concerned with whether I was Tammy! This is actually a very freeing thought. If I am to be me, then I do not have to be worried about who everyone else thinks I should be.

Some people discover their true selves early in life and they are at peace with who they are and what they are doing with their life. For others, the struggle continues. They wrestle with what they should be doing. They follow the road suggested by their parents, spouse, siblings or children with a constant aching feeling in their heart that they should be doing something else.

In many ways, it becomes easier for them to go with the flow than resist the current. Take the safe road. Take the path of least resistance. Walk with the wind. One might even follow society's standards you disagree with simply because it is too much work to resist or stand up for your own standards. How do we begin to gain the confidence we need to become ourselves? Practice. Practice. Practice. This is a concept we learn when we are very young and it should continue throughout our lifetime.

God wants you to be the person he created you to be. He will prompt you, stir your heart, or perhaps whisper to you in the night. Do not let fear, societal pressure, or peer pressure take away your unique personality. Fulfill your obligations and responsibilities as they come along in your life each one helping you uncover who you are, but also remember to be true to yourself and God's purpose for you and you will be more at peace.

Questions to ponder:
How am I living out my purpose in life?
Who limits my personal expression?
What is God calling me to do right now?

Gratitude in All Things

♧♧

For great is your love, higher than the heavens; your
faithfulness reaches to the skies. Be exalted, O God,
above the heavens, and let your glory be over all the
earth. —PSALM 108:4-5

♧♧

As I sat down to write on this particular morning the topic of major discussion in the news was the shortage of flu vaccine. Many people seemed to be in a panic because there was a shortage. A week ago I had heard on the news that some states were considering fining nurses if they gave flu vaccines to individuals whom did not meet the risk criteria. I wanted to hear someone say that they were grateful for the contaminated vaccines being discovered before they were distributed to millions of people. I want to share with you some thoughts about having a grateful heart.

How many of you thought about what could have happened if those contaminated vaccines had not been discovered? How many of you can see God working to protect millions of individuals from potentially serious outcomes? I am so grateful that I did not receive a contaminated vaccine. It is not always easy to be grateful in circumstances that inconvenience us or put us in what we see as potential danger, yet we are called to be grateful in all circumstances and to trust in God. We read in Philippians 4:6, "Do not be anxious about anything, but in everything, by prayer and petition, with *thanksgiving*, present your requests to God", and in Ephesians 5:19, "Speak to one another with psalms, hymns and spiritual songs. Sing and make music in your heart to the Lord, always *giving thanks* to God the Father *for everything*, in the name of our Lord Jesus Christ". Everything? Everything? Even a shortage of vaccines?

I am not sure many people found something to be thankful for in this incident. I was amazed when this shortage in flu vaccines was announced at the panic and need to accuse attitude that broke out. I believe there is a serious quick fix mentality developing in our world. From diets and exercise to financial security, it seems as though everyone wants it now and they want it all, even instant protection from the flu. This troubles me a little; no it troubles me a lot!

I do not believe we can count on our human abilities to always fix our problems, attain security, prevent illness or remove our struggles at the snap of our fingers. Illness and struggle often strengthen us. For example, our immune system from the time we are born develops as we are exposed to illness. When we are exposed to bacteria our body takes note of it so that when we are exposed the next time our body has the ability to identify the bacteria and send out antibodies (protective cells) to fight and destroy the bacteria. My physiology teacher would not be impressed by this simple description of the very intricate immune system, but simply stated we become stronger with exposure. This idea of gaining strength from exposure spills over to include other areas of life as well. Running regularly allows us to become stronger and less winded and financial experiences of the past help us to develop healthy budgets, as other examples.

There are ways in which we can reduce the risk of illness, but it is not always quick or simple. We need to be vigilant in caring for our bodies. Providing our bodies with proper nutrition, hygiene and the rest we need will greatly reduce the risk of illness and strengthen our ability to fight off illness. It is true that flu vaccines provide added support to individuals with compromised immune systems, chronic diseases or poorly developed immune systems, and should be dispensed, but they are not the end all to protecting us against illness. There are after all many other diseases out there. Developing healthy practices can prove beneficial in the long run.

Similarly, our spiritual well being cannot be strong by simply attending a 1-hour worship service on Sunday. Our spirits need and deserve to be nurtured every day. If we are going to combat guilt, practice forgiveness, and resist temptation we need constant nurturing. Gratitude is a profound way to strengthen your spirit. Practicing gratitude assists us in resisting negative, harmful feelings that wound the spirit.

How do we live our lives in gratitude for all things? I have found the best way for me to become more grateful has been to begin and end each day with a prayer of gratitude to God, being grateful for the light of a new day and grateful for the day's end with the setting of the sun. These visual cues have become securely linked to me as times to pause and be grateful. I would say gratitude flows easily from my heart. I know that in the years ahead I may be challenged to find reasons to be thankful for my circumstances. I am confident that by making a conscious effort to identify reasons to be thankful everyday in my life I am strengthening my spirit for times when I may be exposed to illness, loss, or temptation. Having gratitude for a loving God in my heart is the greatest protection I can have.

Ideas for building your gratitude attitude!
Practice gratitude by writing down things you are thankful
for, start by listing 5 things.
Tell those you love that you are thankful for them.
Memorize verses of thanksgiving from your
bible or from authors you enjoy.

*What are some ways you can think of to
strengthen your sense of gratitude?
When faced with difficult circumstances try to find at least
one thing to be thankful for in the situation.*

A Blanket of Warmth

*May the God of hope fill you with all joy and peace as
you trust in him, so that you may overflow with hope by
the power of the Holy Spirit.* —ROMANS 15:13

Bring on spring, please, bring on spring. Writing today under
yet another cloudy sky from which snowflakes are once again
falling, I long for springtime. This winter season seems relentless in dumping snow into our lives. It is almost as if the snowflakes are trying to tell us something. There are so many of them!
If you are up to your ears in snow you may not want to even
think about it another minute, but I invite you to read on for
a new perspective. Let us consider the blanket of warmth the
snow provided us this past winter.

The dark winter days, the driving wind, the heavy snowfalls
mounding up along roadways and sidewalks, and the result-
ant thick blanket of insulation covering the earth has had a
profound effect on many people this winter. Many people have
shared their frustration with me this year over the constant
shoveling, the nagging cold and wicked wind. It certainly has
been a burden for a lot of people. For me, however, I love winter
(strange as that may seem) and wonder what this winter is trying to tell us. It has left many people feeling defeated, worn out,
and exhausted ready to throw in the towel or simply throw their
hands up in the air and say, "I quit". Some people seem to be
shutting down to life.

But the snow reminds us that we must not give up, that we
must keep going. We must clear a path for the mailman to get
through. We must clear the driveway in case of an emergency.

We must keep our sidewalks open to accommodate our neighbors. The workload may seem overwhelming in regard to a new snowfall, but we cannot give up on the task before us. Let's look more closely at these snowflakes.

These snowflakes have the potential to blanket a community together bringing out the best in people. You might find neighbors helping one another clear off driveways and sidewalks. You might find that at a four-way stop drivers are more willing to motion for the other vehicle to go first. You might notice when someone is approaching the corner of the street not yet into the crosswalk drivers will stop and wait for them to cross smiling as the individual waves a thank you for letting them get on their way and out of the weather only that much sooner.

Families are given the opportunity to share the blanket of warmth as they gather around a table to play a game or bundle up to go out and play together; laughing, diving into the snow or sliding down the hill, catching snowflakes on your tongue as they fall, or peering through snowflake laden lashes for a fresh view of the world.

The pure white blanket of snow insulates the world. Plants are given time to gain strength for the coming season. Could it be that the snow is a reminder for each of us to search out ways to gain strength for the season of life we are in the midst of right now? Another question to consider as the snow continues to fall is this, what does it tell us about purity. We read in Psalm 51:7, "Purify me from my sins, and I will be clean; wash me, and I will be whiter than snow". This statement identifies snow as being an object of purity. A blanket of snow can remind us of God's pure unending love and the freedom his forgiveness affords us. The newness provided when we seek forgiveness and of God's desire to call each of us into a relationship of pure love with him.

The burden of a snowfall can be heavy, but regardless of the heaviness in our lives, the relentless cold we might be facing, we must forge forward and clear the path to our future gaining strength as we go. At times in our life we may face a giant snowfall that seems to weigh us down, but we must remember our Creator God allows us to use all things in life to prepare us for what we may need in the days ahead. May the blanket of snow upon the earth remind you of a big white blanket of warmth sent down as a sign of God's pure unending love and promised strength for the future.

Questions to ponder:
What does snow represent in my life, burden,
blanket, purity?
How do I manage the heavy snowfalls on my life journey?
How do the burdens in life unite communities?

CHAPTER 3

Facing Our Fears

೪೭

And only when we are no longer afraid do we begin to live in every experience, painful or joyous; to live in gratitude for every moment, to live abundantly.
—*DOROTHY THOMPSON*

Listening For the Echo

ﾐﾐ

The awesome Power of God
The awesome Power of God
The awesome Power of God

ﾐﾐ

I experienced firsthand a deep sense of peace coming from the compassion of the many individuals caring for our family. It had been through their compassionate hearts that I was able to fully witness the Power of One. I have heard the echo. I invite you to reflect with me on this topic, listening for the echo.

When your fear is great what do *you* do? The first thing I do is ask God to take away my fear. Then *I call* someone to tell them about my fear. Perhaps in some ways I am looking for them to remove my fear even after I have offered it to God and know full well that he is the only one powerful enough to remove my fear. It is, however, exactly what I do. I call someone so that I can hear a voice. It is what I have found myself doing during a family crisis. I offered my fear to God, asked him to remove my fear, and then called a long list of people to ask for their help. I needed to pray and I needed their prayers.

I wonder if I thought God would hear someone else's prayer better than my own. Did I think if I asked enough people to pray it would be like turning up the volume? God would certainly hear my need if I got enough volume behind it. I dialed one number after the other asking for prayers.

My body had responded appropriately to my fear. I felt nauseous, sweaty yet cold, my mouth was dry, pretty much text book! It was my spirit that kept nudging me to make another call. Then it occurred to me the calls were needed as a support for my spirit. Each person granted me a compassionate ear and offered to pray for healing and peace.

Even as I knelt in the chapel praying fervently I found myself dialing the phone again. I recalled the words found in Matthew 18:20, "For where there are two or three gathered together in my name there I am in the midst of them." I guess I felt that having a friend on the phone with me would fulfill this promise. It was at that time that I realized the depth of compassion being poured forth from others. Their care and concern for my family echoed God's response to my initial prayer request. The words being echoed were these, Tammy, sometimes I will calm the storm and sometimes I will calm you. Instantly the words of the song by Scott Krippayne, *Sometimes He Calms the Storm*, came rushing into my head. The song describes the power of God to either calm the storm or calm the child with the assurance that indeed he will do one or the other. They kept repeating in my head.

I had not heard his response on my own. It needed to be echoed through the compassion of others. I realized what God was telling me was that these circumstances required a storm, a storm against an infection. What he needed me to do was remain calm and with a calm spirit I was better equipped to be a prayer warrior for my loved one. My renewed, engaged spirit remained calm and allowed me to be an instrument for the awesome power of God. Slowly and methodically I prayed for my loved one and 0.1 point at a time the storm (a raging fever) was calmed by the mighty hand of God.

As I wrote this reflection the storm continued. New waves of symptoms presented themselves and I was reminded to listen for the echo. I opened to the echoing message coming through the compassionate hearts of others. Listen for the echoes in your life. The compassionate hearts around you are echoing the power God in your life journey.

Questions to ponder:
When has the storm raged in my life?
Who echoed God's calming message to me?
How am I an instrument of calm in for someone else?

Embracing the Struggle

୨୧

God's ways are always right. They may not make sense to us. They may be mysterious, inexplicable, difficult, and even painful. But they are right. —MAX LUCADO

୨୧

All around me there is evidence of spring. All around me there is evidence of growth. All around me there is rejoicing in accomplishment and survival. And in the midst of all of this evidence is a sense of struggle. I cannot describe the depth of struggle in terms of level or degrees because it is unique to that for which the struggle is occurring. In this reflection consider the struggles in life and more importantly the possibility of embracing the struggle.

My husband and I planted some fruit trees on our property. We live in a very windy area and therefore we staked these trees for support knowing they would struggle to stay upright in the wind as they began to set down roots in their new location. Months later we were talking about whether to leave the stakes in or remove them. I was thinking to myself, what would be the harm in supporting them through the year, when my husband said, "If we support them too long they won't develop deep roots". Of course, the trees will not be allowed to struggle against the wind, which would drive their root system deeper and ultimately increase the strength of the tree. Without strength, how would they support their fruit? How would they stand tall against a storm?

So it is with us, if we are allowed to struggle our roots, our faith goes deep and becomes our source of strength. I fear there have been times when I have mistakenly thought by holding someone else up in their struggle I was giving them the best opportunity to withstand the struggle they were up against, the wind pushing them down. Have you ever felt as though you needed to come to the rescue of someone who was in the midst of a struggling relationship, financial difficulties, or a poor life-style choice? What I am considering now is that although my desire to help others and my deep compassion for people's circumstances is part of who I am, I must consider that if I try to remove the need for struggle from them I could in the long run be causing them harm, weakening their root system.

I had been reading a book by Joan D. Chittister entitled, *Scarred by Struggle, Transformed by Hope*, an excellent book, and she says this about struggle, "If we are willing to persevere through the depths of struggle we can emerge with conversion, independence, faith, courage, surrender, self-acceptance, endurance, purity of heart and a kind of personal growth that takes us beyond pain to understanding. Enduring struggle is the price to be paid for becoming everything we are meant to be in the world". All of these pieces had been lining up, springtime, windy days, to stake or not to stake, reading this passage, so that I could see in myself that I needed to adjust the ways I care for others so that I can be more supportive of their personal growth. I also needed to consider the importance of embracing my personal struggles as important for helping me to become all that I am meant to be in this world.

In some way I am being called to be with struggle rather than defeat struggle. Instead of trying to find ways to remove struggle from my life or from someone else's life I am being encouraged to explore what the struggle means, what potential growth lies in the struggle, what good can come from it? There are dramatic examples of struggle in our world that remind us of the good that can come. Consider the birth of a baby, labor is certainly a struggle. A baby brings joy. Consider the release of a butterfly from its cocoon certainly a struggle. The butterfly brings beauty to our world.

Every day we are exposed to various forms of struggle, to get to work on time, to find a job, to get out of bed in the morning, to lose a few pounds, to say no to a risky behavior, to accept an unfulfilled dream. Every day there are people wanting to help and we need to accept their help to a certain extent. Beyond that we need to embrace our struggle trusting that God will be our ultimate strength in the struggle and that whether we understand at the time or not we will one day be able to understand that the struggle we experienced was part of growing into the person we were meant to be. I believe we will one day see the good that comes from embracing the struggle.

Questions to ponder:
What struggles am I experiencing in my life?
How have others helped me?
Have I embraced the struggle for the good it might bring to my life?

False Evidence Appearing Real

❧

So do not fear, for I am with you; do not be dismayed, for
I am your God.
I will strengthen you and help you; I will uphold you
with my righteous right hand. —ISAIAH 41:10

❧

In the summer of 2010 I took up running or jogging I should say and to this day I still question what I was thinking! Well even more amazing to me a year later was that I found myself training for a 1/4 marathon. All in all this activity has been a lesson in perseverance, but on this particular morning in May I learned something about facing fear. Let me share with you what I discovered about fear or as a friend described, False Evidence Appearing Real.

I had decided to do my run early in the morning as it is usually less windy early in the morning and I very much dislike running in the wind. It takes my breath away and I am always afraid I will have to stop before I reach my goal, not that doing so would be the worst thing, but in trying to increase my endurance I was afraid I would lose confidence if I had to stop. Well on that particular morning when I was scheduled to do my longest run before the event I found myself meeting face to face with my fear. The wind was up and running early! Oh, there was plenty of evidence. The flag was whipping practically straight out, the branches were swaying, and the grass on the lawn was visibly straining to stand upright.

The wind gusts made an eerie howl like a voice telling me I would fail. The wind seemed to call out, "You are not strong enough". My physical senses took over. Hearing the sound of the wind, imagining the feeling of the pressure on my lungs, seeing the driving force against nature all created a deep sense of fear within me. I started to agree with my fear and resigned to stay inside. My spirit screamed as loud as it could, "Don't give in. Fear wants you to give in. The evidence is false. I can prove it. You are strong. I am your strength. Call on me. I am right here". How quickly I had fallen victim to my fear.

I had to ask myself this question, 'what if it is really windy the day of the run and I am not prepared'? 'What then'? I gathered myself together, put on my shoes and out the door I went willing to face my fear, preparing myself for unexpected times of trial. As I ran into the wind I knew I was in for a fight. It was amazing how physically winded I became just hearing the sound of the wind whistling through the trees, almost taunting me with an occasional gust. My legs cried out, my lungs were burning, but deep within my spirit, waiting once again to be called into the game to help, whispered, "Call on me, call on me".

So, I did. My spirit was there to remind me that I am never alone in the struggle. I am never alone in accomplishing my hopes and dreams. As I ran I was reminded that many times I am lured away from the things I want to do, things I should do, things I dream to do, because of fear. I discovered or perhaps once again uncovered the reality that fear has the ability to steal my joy. Steal my strength. Steal my dreams.

My spirit helped me conquer my fear and transform it from a paralyzing force into an energizing force that helped me finish my run. I began to smile and thanked my fear for showing me how important my spirit is to me. For showing me that I must exercise my spirit regularly so that in the event I am faced with a surprising situation I will be ready for it.

Listen to your spirit. It is calling out words of encouragement when you face your fears reminding you that you are not alone in your struggles. Your spirit wants to be called into the game to transform false evidence appearing real into positive energy that propels you forward to follow your dreams and meet the challenges of life.

Questions to ponder:
Have I ever fallen victim to my fear(s)?
Is there False Evidence Appearing Real in my life?
Does it prevent me from setting my goals high, prevent me from reconciling with a family member or friend, or prevent me from reaching for my dreams?

It's Not _ _ _ _, is it?

❧❧

2009-A Prayer against the H1N1 Virus

H-ear our cry against you
1-you will not break my spirit
N-or will I be driven from helping others
1-with Christ we will be healed

❧❧

It is with hesitation that I begin this reflection to all of you, because it is about a topic that has already gotten too much press in my estimation, but I believe God has something to say about all of this and is moving my fingers in an effort to be heard. There is something very troubling to me in regard to the upcoming flu season. The media is filling our heads with a lot of scare tactics and people are responding with anxiety and near paranoia. I want to reflect with you about caring for the sick regardless whether it is _ _ _ _, or not.

During this time of heavy media attention to the topic I found myself feeling sick. It was the typical fall sinus headache with drainage down the back of my throat making my throat sore with some coughing due to the irritation in my throat. Remembering that just the week before I had spoken to a group of children and their teachers about what to do when you get the flu and that I had advised them that they should stay home from school or work if they had symptoms I determined that I should stay home from work. Rest is after all the best medicine for combating most types of illness. Well, I developed laryngitis. As you can imagine, however, when I returned to work my voice was still quite gruff. Frankly, I sounded awful when I greeted people. What do you suppose was the reaction I received from most people? Yup, they would slightly step back and say, "it isn't _ _ _ _ is it? I wonder what they would have done if I would have said, "yes, by the way it is _ _ _ _, thank you for asking?

We seem to have this idea that the H 1 N 1 virus is the worst thing in the world. Please do not misunderstand me here; this virus needs to be taken seriously, just like any other virus needs to be taken seriously. Bacterial infections need to be taken seriously. Sedentary life style needs to be taken seriously. Walking across the street in busy traffic needs to be taken seriously. Sorry, I was climbing onto my soap box.

I wonder if we as a society have become so laissez faire about our healthcare system taking care of us that we believe we do not have to take care of ourselves or others,? There have always been sick people around us. In the grocery stores. On the street. In the church pew. Why have we all of the sudden decided we need to protect ourselves? Why do we suddenly seem to believe that we are more important than the person across the street? Where is the compassionate caring going to come from in all of this?

I have fears, too. Certainly, I have always feared the flu. Many people die every year from complications of the flu. I have always known people dear to me that are at higher risk for complications of the flu. I have been praying for all those individuals long before the onset of this projected pandemic. The H1N1 virus is not an automatic death sentence, but the way we were responding to it seemed certainly to be a death sentence for the human spirit.

The flu season of 2009 was no different than any other flu season in regard to prevention. Good hand washing, staying home when you are sick, staying away from others who are at high risk for complications, using and disposing of tissues/handkerchiefs, and staying healthy by eating right, exercising and getting your rest will be your best defense against any flu virus, bacterial infection, or even accidental injury. I believe it is, however, our spiritual health and the spiritual health of our communities that will be most difficult to support if we continue to maintain the "I", "me" position. We must unite and place ourselves in the presence of God and respond to the direction he leads us, caring for others who are sick without fear of becoming ill ourselves.

I find comfort in the Psalms and as I read this passage I thought it applied to our current circumstance, "I am praying to you because I know you will answer, O God. Bend down and listen as I pray. Show me your unfailing love in wonderful ways. You save with your strength those who seek refuge from their enemies. Guard me as the apple of your eye. Hide me in the shadow of your wings" Psalm 17:6-8.

Our vaccines, our methods of prevention, our determination to stay healthy will all be amplified with prayer. Let us join our voices in prayer to the God who created us. We can become broken down by the negative press or united and lifted up as we combat our afflictions as one Spirit in Christ.

Questions to ponder:
When has fear and panic caused my spirit to be burdened?
How has the media falsely portrayed
circumstances in my life?
How can I turn the "I", "Me" mentality into "We"?

Weathering the Storm

 споре

*Spiritual Hunger Can it be? Have I for so long forgotten
to feed myself? Yes. For nigh a year now I was starving.
Getting lost in busy days, tossing aside the hunger that
chewed away inside. Yet, I did not die. By some quiet
miracle I made it to this moment of truth: I nearly
starved to death. It was not my body that I failed to feed.
It was my spirit, left alone for days without nourishment or care. And then one day I paused to look within,
shocked at what I found: so thin of faith, so weak of
understanding, so needy of encouragement. My starving
spirit cried the truth: I can! I will! I must be fed! Catho-
lic Health Association of Wisconsin, SOURCE UNKNOWN*

споре

I am waiting for yet another storm of the season. With the fore-
cast of a winter storm we often plan ahead for being unable to
leave our homes during the storm. There is a message that comes
in preparing for a winter storm. It speaks to us in regard to the
storms of life. I want to share with you my thoughts on being
prepared to weather the storm.

Throughout life we may encounter events that cause us to
stop in our tracks. Stop! Totally stop! Suddenly there is nothing, nothing more important than the event being faced. We
are challenged to rapidly re-prioritize our life. When we know
a winter storm is coming we get ready for it. We prepare ahead.
We stock the cupboards with groceries. We place blankets, hats,
mittens, a shovel, sandbags and flashlights in our vehicles. We
arm ourselves for enduring the storm.

How do we arm ourselves for the storms of life? Where do we get the necessary supplies for weathering the storms of life? Our greatest resources come from our spirituality. However, our resources may be more scattered than those organized on shelving in the grocery store. They may be depleted, exhausted. They may be non-existent. We may feel spiritually empty. How do we ensure that our spirituality is stocked and ready to face the storms of life? We must find effective ways to tend to our spiritual needs. Taking time to deepen our understanding of what causes our spirit to feel healthy. Ensuring that we carry out activities to maintain a healthy spirit is imperative.

Personal life storms, although sometimes predictable are often unpredictable. They can come out of nowhere. The longer we live the more aware we are of the fact that storms will affect each of us at sometime in our life. We need to be prepared for the storms of life. We tend to move along in life, perhaps beginning slowly, but then surging forward with the day-to-day activities and leadings of society sometimes unaware that our spiritual stores are being depleted. We may find ourselves drifting further away from our spiritual source. My relationship with God is the ultimate source for strengthening my spirituality and making my way through the painful storms of life. Often it is in times of great need for the supportive love of God, that we feel miles away from this loving source of strength and I believe it is because we have become too comfortable with the status quo. Sadly, "everything is going fine, thanks God", becomes our only interaction, conversation, or prayer with God.

I wonder how strong my relationship with God would be today if I fell into the day-to-day pace and offered only a simple, "everything is going fine, thanks God". As my memory serves me, there was a time when I didn't offer much more than this to my relationship with God. I shudder to think how painful life experiences would be had I not realized the importance of nurturing and strengthening this relationship.

Today, my days start with prayers for strength to face the challenges of the day, guidance to know what God would see as being the most important activity of the day, and patience in my inadequacy. I pray for family and friends in the activities they will be doing throughout their day. I have conversations with God off and on all day long and at the end of my day, I offer prayers of thanksgiving for the day and the interactions I had with others.

Each of us needs to develop our own spiritual practices. I shared some of my daily routine in an effort to dispel the misconception that the only way to have a relationship with God is to memorize his word. I believe that knowing his word helps me to converse openly with God throughout the day, but it is not the only conversation to have with him. The bible strengthens our faith, shares God's promises with us, and propels us into action. Knowing God's word alone, however, is not the only ingredient in developing a strong relationship with God.

Your connectedness with God comes from the conversations you have on a regular, relaxed basis. It is the kind of relationship that prepares you for the storms of life. When you have no doubt about where God is in any given moment you begin to prepare yourself for the storms of life. Like waiting for a snowstorm, which causes us to consider our resources and stock up for a long siege of being homebound, a strong relationship with God provides us with a comfort level of knowing that somewhere in the storms of our life God is working to hold us together, to prepare us for the next step, to give us unconditional love, to forgive us for our mistakes.

For me, God is the ultimate resource for handling the storms of life and I know this from the experiences I have had with others as they encounter storms I cannot even imagine traveling through. Yet their ability to go forward is often visible to me as God holding them closely and walking with them or carrying them gently in his arms.

I pray for God to deepen my spirituality and strengthen my relationship with him that I might be prepared to weather the storms I will encounter. With each storm that comes along I become more motivated to plan ahead. It is hard to run out and get a loaf of bread when snow or ice covers the road so you and I pick the loaf up on the way home just in case the weatherman is right! Likewise it is hard to hold onto a stranger for strength so I encourage you to not let God be a stranger. Stock you spiritual resources. You will need this spiritual strength when the storms of life blow your direction.

Questions to ponder:
What storms have I encountered in life?
Was I prepared?
How will I plan ahead for future storms of life?

Procrastination

❧❧

Call to me and I will answer you and tell you great and unsearchable things you do not know. —JEREMIAH 33:3

❧❧

Even as I sit here at the computer I am doing the very thing I intend to write about. Procrastinating! What is it with procrastination? Although I would describe myself as organized, the kind of person who likes to have things done ahead of time there are still times like the present when I find myself procrastinating about something I have to do. I am attributing this morning's feeling to God's true desire for me to write to you about procrastination.

Self-discovery can be painful. As I prepare this letter to all of you this morning I am seeing many of my own characteristics of procrastination. I do realize those of you who know me well know that I am never early to meetings and I must admit that is probably a prime example of procrastination, which I am sure you are all nodding your heads about. Right? I know, I know, but it hurts when you discover things about yourself that you would rather not call your own personality traits. Yet, there is learning with every discovery. Thank you all once again for giving me time for self-reflection, discovery and learning. So I encourage all of you to ponder with me this topic of procrastination. As you are reading I imagine you are wondering if I am ever going to get to the topic. Exactly! Procrastination abounds!

Why do we procrastinate? What keeps us from getting on with things we know we have to do, want to do, or dream about doing? I do not have a concrete answer for this question. There are I suppose as many answers as there are individuals. Today, fear presents itself as perhaps my biggest reason for procrastinating. I used to think that I put some things off because I enjoyed the slight pressure that comes with having a deadline, the surge of adrenaline that comes with necessity for completing something at the last minute. This morning to be fully honest with myself I must admit fear is the most likely culprit in my procrastination. The fear of writing something that is not worth reading. Fear of not being good enough. Fear of failure. Fear.

I have heard it said that fear is false (f), evidence (e), appearing (a), real(r). I like this description and have perhaps used it in my reflections before (and likely will again). False evidence. God has written all of my other letters in the past why do I think he will fail me now? There is no evidence of his leaving me high and dry without a topic or message of encouragement to write for you to read. It is all imagined. Not true.

You might be saying to yourself, well fear doesn't describe procrastination in regard to my work. Or does it? Even if the task we are putting off is a small job around the house perhaps the thought of having something to do allows us to put off the fear of having nothing to do, having time on our hands. What then? What will do if we get this project done? Is fear of the unknown future a motivation for your procrastination? If we hang on to our procrastination then we always have something to do. Does this make sense? Let's look at it in an example.

The little things like doing the dishes, doing the laundry, or dusting the furniture may not have great consequences in and of themselves if put off, but the bigger or harder things in life, like talking with a friend who hurt you, apologizing for something you did wrong, giving time for someone who is in need or taking those first steps toward a lifelong dream are put off just a little longer when we can say that we do not have time because we still have dishes, laundry or dusting to do.

Now many things in life cause us to put off our dreams, our projects, or our work. What God is asking me to share with all of you is that no matter what your reasons are your spirit is calling you to do something that will be worthwhile for you, your life, or your loved ones. No matter how many excuses you come up for putting it off, your spirit will steer you back to the thing you need to do. So do it!

God will speak to you on your own issues of procrastination as you read this letter if you allow him to. My examples are simple, but your situation may be deeper. Listen to your spirit. *Listen* to your spirit. Are you being called to do something? Go ahead. Get started. If it were not important God would not be calling you to it. He would not keep calling you to do it. Just the mere fact that you are being called should be support enough in knowing that God is already there with you. God is calling you because he wants to support you in your efforts. Draw strength from the spirit within you to take one step at a time in the direction of completion.

As for me, procrastination will come on occasion without a doubt, but God has written a letter of encouragement on my heart and I have shared it with you. God has called my spirit to this task and has completed it through me. May you find comfort in the words he has written?

Questions to ponder:
What is God calling me to do?
What is my greatest fear?

CHAPTER 4

Releasing Control

%

*Prayer of Discernment, By <u>Joyce Rupp (from her book</u>
<u>Out of the Ordinary)</u>*

*Spirit of Guidance, I see before me numerous choices and a deci-
sion to be made. There is division in my heart. Sometimes I want
none of what I find. Sometimes I want it all. Sometimes I want
to give up making decisions and wish that the future would go
away. I entrust my decision-making into your hands, ready to
do my part but also knowing that I cannot do this without your
help. Lead me through all the unsure, unclear, doubtful, hesitant,
and questioning moments that are mine as I search to find the
right way in which to go. Grant me the grace to choose freely,
without being attached to the outcome. I trust that you will be*

with me as I make my decision prayerfully and with faith. Assure me that your peace will rest deep within me as I make the decision that seems best for me at this time. I may continue to experience feelings of turmoil and confusion, but deep within I know that I can return to that settled place in me where you always dwell. Guide and Director of my life, I place my life in your hands. Lead me to the path that will best deepen and strengthen my relationship with you.

Think For Yourself

℘℘

Listen for the messages God *is sending you...*

℘℘

In the midst of winter's gradual thaw I found myself bouncing back and forth between two topics. Each seems to have equal importance. One aligns with the calendar season and one aligns with this season of our life. Which one will I expound on? Well, knowing that the seasonal calendar is unpredictable in Wisconsin, I will hold that topic for another time and settle in on the topic addressing the current season of life.

A few weeks ago, while listening to the Christian radio station, a renowned speaker was giving some advice. I have typically agreed with his encouraging words, but this particular day I was not in agreement. I actually (although I don't have too much hair on the back of my neck) felt the hair on the back of my neck stand at attention. In summary, he described a small bible study group. He asked whether we had ever experienced sitting around discussing a section of the bible with questions about its meaning. He commented that likely there would be responses such as; "I don't know" or "well, my grandpa used to say" (aren't those common responses when we begin to understand the meaning of anything in life?). Then he went on to imply that this was a bad approach to learning about God and that we should trust our study to those who have completed education around the topic and not waste our time pondering questions. It sounded like he did not want us to think for ourselves. The world seems a little like that right now, in this season of life.

If I would have relied solely on educated theologians for learning about God I would not have had the depth of experience in developing a relationship with God that I have been blessed with. I would venture to say that my spiritual wellbeing would be stagnant. I would have learned my prayers, settled into a weekly routine of attending church and sat quietly while I was fed the ideas of another person.

What my spirit needed to become healthy was to ask questions, to ask those who have received advanced education in theology, to ask aging relatives, to ask friends, and to ask myself to be open to listening for the voice of God in my everyday life, in my everyday experiences.

I am not willing to pass judgment (as this person was doing) on someone's depth of understanding God's plan for their life being based on their *teacher*. The *teacher* in my mind is God. If I do not think about his word myself, if I rely only on the interpretation of another, I limit my relationship. I believe I distance my relationship. It seems to me that there are too many people in the world today trying to take away our ability to think for ourselves. That is a dangerous place to be. Complacency sets in. We become uncreative. We become unresponsive to life. We become spiritually bankrupt.

God has something to say to you. He will use many avenues to reach you. He will use education. He will us church services. He will use bible studies hosted in individual's homes. But, let's not forget that he will use the silence. He will use his word quietly pondered or openly discussed with others. He will provide you with experiences to deepen your inner desire to know more, to have a better understanding, to have a stronger personal relationship with him.

Listen. Read. Ask questions. Listen for answers. Ponder the responses. Think for yourself. Then ask God if you are on the right track, **he** is ready to lead you in the right direction.

Questions to ponder:
Has anyone ever told me what I should think?
How did I respond to them?
When will I spend time listening for the messages God is
sending me?

Set a Goal

❧❧

"Therefore, since we are surrounded by such a huge crowd of witnesses to the life of faith, let us strip off every weight that slows us down, especially the sin that so easily hinders our progress. And let us run with endurance the race that God has set before us. We do this by keeping our eyes on Jesus, on whom our faith depends from start to finish..." —HEBREWS 12:1-2

❧❧

I have received an important message from a seemingly simple activity, goal setting. One summer I began a new venture in an effort to increase my physical stamina. I began to jog. I began to jog? This is not something I would ever want to do. Did I really take up jogging? I did and it has not only increased my stamina it has increased my faith. Let me explain to you what I have come to learn by setting a goal.

One day I decided to go for a (my) jog (I jog?). I started off and it occurred to me that it was the first time since I took up this little activity that I was not overcome with doubts. This was new. So, I decided to jog 3 miles that morning. I usually found myself thinking, 'well maybe I will first try to jog to that next pole', and 'if I am not tired then I will jog to the next pole', but if I am tired at the next pole I am definitely stopping. This is silly, I would think to myself. Then I would question why I needed to do this activity anyway? Believe me I could talk myself into giving up the goal almost before I set out to accomplish it. This day was different.

I began to jog feeling a newfound strength in my breath, a confidence in placing one foot in front of the other, a deep sense that I was not jogging alone. I felt the presence of my spirit's will to accomplish this goal. God was with me even in this activity. When I kept my focus on God's desire for me to meet my goal I felt strong. When I faltered toward doubt I began to feel weak. The goal was to jog for 3 miles (no big deal for many of you, but for those of you who know me or have seen me jog, it was a lofty goal). God was guiding me toward the completion of my goal all the way to the finish line.

There are often things in life we do not want to do, may never think ourselves capable of doing, but without a goal and a plan for achieving that goal we never have the opportunity to praise God for attaining it. What happens when you cross the finish line, reach the top of the hill (or mountain), complete the project at work, or make the connection with a friend or family member you have not seen in a long time? What happens? You rejoice! You celebrate! You do a little dance and your spirit smiles. You are well within. You experience a great sense of peace.

Here is the message, the lesson in spiritual wellness I learned that day. We need to have goals. We need to have something to strive toward. It stretches our spirit, invigorates our spirit, it highlights our spirit. Have you ever noticed that we call on God when we want to get something done? God is in the conversation the minute we set a goal. More than once I have heard people say, "God willing I will get this done". More than once I have prayed, 'Lord, let me accomplish the goals you have set for me this day', 'give me a reason, a purpose for living in this place and time'. 'Give me a goal'.

Does that mean that any goal I set will be accomplished? Not necessarily. I think goals should be true to our calling. I am really quite sure that God has not called me to be a marathon runner, but perhaps he has called me to do something I did not want to do in order that I might be reminded that it is not about me doing it anyway. It is about what God can do. It is about God working through me to accomplish the work he has laid out for me to do.

I set out that morning to accomplish a goal of jogging 3 miles; God ran it with me to prove to me that he is in it through the tough stuff and that I can meet my goals one step at a time. Set a goal. Take that step. Trust God on the journey to completion. Your spirit is just waiting to cross that finish line with a smile.

Questions to ponder:
What goals do I have in life?
Has God called me to something I am not sure I can do?
How will I trust God to help me accomplish my goals?

What to Do With the Silence

୧୧

Be still and know that I am God. —PSALM 46:10

୧୧

As I write to you today my room is silent. I can only hear the distant sound of a clock ticking. Silence is a beautiful sound. That may seem contradictory, yet I believe that the silence speaks to us. I want to encourage you to listen to the silence.

We live in a world of noise and activity. Many people are not comfortable in a room when silence enters. They jump in to break the silence. Perhaps they even fear the silence. Quite often I have seen people wish they would have kept quiet during those times of silence because as a result of their fears they jumped in and said something they wish they would not have said.

Have you ever sat in a silent room and began to imagine things that were not real? How many times have you been sure that someone was knocking on the door only to find that the sound was related to the furnace or refrigerator? There is something about silence that creates fear and suspicion. It is often a time of questioning where God is. There are times in life when God seems very near. Whether it is during celebration or in times of sorrow, we can still sense the presence of God. But what do we do with the silent times when God seems far away.

As I look over the past year I have experienced times of silence. I noticed during those times that I could allow the silence to exist for a while, but soon my response would become filled with questions about what God was trying to tell me. What direction was I suppose to take? What should I do to hear God's message better? I was trying to fill the silence. As the questions filled my mind fear entered and with fear present in my mind my physical being began to respond negatively. It was interesting to consider what was causing my fear. It was the silence. It was during times when I felt God was not speaking to me, not directing me. I was trying go it alone, impatient in the silence.

Now, silence has been a friend to me over the years and I was not happy with myself for allowing fear to enter my life and take away the beauty of silence. It is during silent times in our lives that we can most clearly see ourselves. We are not wrapped up in all the things we should be doing for other people and we can begin to see what we need to do for ourselves.

A dear friend of mine sent me a card once when I was experiencing one of those silent times years ago that I have framed and displayed in my office. It has become one of my favorite bible messages. Psalm 46:10 tells us to "Be still and know that I am God". Be still. Be silent. This statement has few words yet the message is so powerful. I believe it is telling me that the silence will provide me with what I need and by knowing that God is in the silence I need not have fear in my heart. Sometimes I forget what I know to be so true (framing the verse helps!).

As I waited for a message to share with you this month I began to think I was not going to have a topic. God was not sending me anything. Then in the night I woke thinking about his silence and there was a song running through my head. The lyrics of the song, *You Are Mine* by David Haas, that were reeling in my mind were, "I will come to you in the silence, I will lift you from all your fear, you will hear my voice, I claim you as my choice, be still and know I am here". In other words I was to write to you about silence and the reassurance that God will not desert you or me, but that he is present in the silence.

So what do you do in the silence? You wait. In the presence of others or in the quiet space in your home it is okay to remain silent. As I mentioned earlier, if we rush in to break the silence we might say something we will regret. If we become impatient we may interrupt the message that God is trying to send us.

This reflection letter comes to you as encouragement to not fear the times when God seems silent in your life, but to welcome the silence as a way to listen to what it might be that you need in your life. Consider creating a space in your home where you can sit in silence for a few moments every day. Become comfortable in the silence and it will truly become a beautiful sound.

Questions to ponder:
Where can I create a silent space in my life?
How have I viewed silence in the past?
How will I embrace silent times?

The Author and the Storyteller

☙☙

"For I know the plans I have for you", declares the Lord,
"plans to prosper you and not to harm you, plans to give
you a hope and a future". —JEREMIAH 29:11

☙☙

Every year I wait for spring to come into full bloom and every year I know it will unfold before me and I will stand in wonder and awe. Isn't that is the way our personal story unfolds, with wonder and awe? Sometimes I cannot wait to know what is going to happen next, or how things will come together. But the ending is not mine to write. God writes the story. My job is to tell it. I want to reflect with you about trusting the author and being the storyteller.

I had found myself over the course of 10 days or so planning my life story. I had anticipated the outcomes, daily. I planned to do this activity in case this happens and that activity in case that happened. I was constantly aware of the fact that my plans could change at any minute, realizing I could not know the minute, yet wanting to desperately. As I looked back over those last 10 days, I questioned why things had not gone the way I planned. There were open spaces of time that would have been perfect for the events of my life to align. Yes, they would have been perfect, or so I thought.

As I walked the Lord reminded me that I am not the author, I am the storyteller. The story is being written and I must be patient for the details. My anticipation and preparation over those 10 days had not been wasted. Those days provided me with a concrete message, which has 2 important points; be ready and trust the author.

I do not know what will happen today, tonight or tomorrow, but I must be aware that my life can change at any time. I must pay attention to my personal health, my faith, my family, my job, my community. I am on call for life. I worked in the operating room for 9 years and was on call from time to time. During my periods of call I would have to be ready to drop what I was doing and go immediately to the hospital. I remember there were times when I almost forgot I was carrying a beeper. I had become comfortable with being on call and responding as needed. Never once did I know how many times the beeper would go off during that time. Never once did I know what I was going to be doing when the call came.

Life is not so different from carrying a beeper. We do not know where we will be when we may need to be called away from our work, project or event. We need to be ready to respond to the events of our life as they unfold. I do not regret my busy preparations over those 10 days in anticipation of being called away because I had the comfort of knowing that I would be ready whenever. I believe being ready has more to do with our relationship with God than with the activities of daily living, but that is another story.

Let my get back to this story. I must trust the author of the story. I do believe that God is the author of my life. I believe this with all of my heart. But, occasionally I try to write a chapter or two and I am reminded that I am not the author. God is the author and even when it seems as though he is taking a break from writing my story, when the anticipation is so high in my heart (as it was those 10 days waiting for our 4th grandchild to be born), I must remember that good stories unfold over time. If I rush through the details of my life, I will miss so much. With every story there are details you miss if you read too fast. You can miss the points of wonder and awe. Life like a good story needs to unfold slowly with anticipation.

My story is continuing to unfold and I wait for the details of today to be my direction for tomorrow. I am thankful for this reminder that all is well in the author's plan for my life story. I cannot read ahead nor can I help with this chapter. It is so wonderful for me to think about how God sends me messages to share with you. Yesterday, as I wrote to a colleague outlining preparation for a retreat, which I may or may not be able to attend depending on my unfolding story, I ended my note to her with these words; I cannot wait to see how God unfolds this story.

Each of you has a story to tell. God is unfolding your story every minute of the day. Be aware of the trust you have in the author of your life story and tell the story of this trusting relationship between the author and the storyteller.

Questions to ponder:
How often do I try to write my own story?
How has God altered the chapters of my life?
Who can I share my life story with?

Deep Cleaning

❧❧

This is the day the Lord has made; let us rejoice and be glad in it. —PSALM 118:24

❧❧

It was a cold day of winter and I found myself at home with nothing on the calendar. There was no place I had to be. No work I needed to do at home. My husband was off to work. It occurred to me that I should do some house cleaning. I am not talking about the regular weekly house cleaning. I am talking about the deep cleaning where you throw things out that are cluttering your life. I invite you to reflect with me on the topic of deep cleaning.

I soon felt the pangs of drudgery. The daunting task before me of sorting through items tucked in my drawers and cupboards that were no longer useful, yet for some reason I was having difficulty discarding, seemed a bit overwhelming. I tried to distract myself with other things. Perhaps I should do some baking? No, I did not have any baking needs and more importantly I don't even like to bake. Perhaps I could start a sewing project? I like to sew, but I really did not have anything in mind. I was stalling. Perhaps I would read for the day? My spirit called out to me urging me not to procrastinate any longer. I had a job to do. It was right there in front of me and I had the time to do it. I simply needed to get to it.

I asked God to give me a cheerful heart in accomplishing this task. Soon I was in my glory! I was sorting and scrubbing, organizing and flinging. It felt so good to have space in the cupboard, empty slots in the drawers. Coats were washed, boots were shined. The music was turned up and I was having a great time. Then it occurred to me that my spirit was dancing. It felt lighter, joyful, and genuinely happy.

How does this topic of deep cleaning relate to your life? Well think about it. Are there things in your heart that you hold onto that are taking up space? Do these things prevent you from taking in more love? Often times we carry hurts in our heart that block our ability to love again, someone hurt us with harsh words, a friend forgets to call, a neighbor borrows something and does not return it. We hold onto things as if they have some benefit for us. They don't. Just like the bottles of lotion, which I thought I liked the fragrance of, that, sit three quarters full in the back of my cupboard, these things are useless.

The things we hold onto in our hearts should be useful in fulfilling our spiritual joy. They should not be there taking up space that could be used for praising God. Psalm 51:10 reads, "Create in me a pure heart, O God, and renew a steadfast spirit within me." There is a beautiful song by Donnie McClurkin on this very topic. It is titled, *Create in Me a Clean Heart* and the refrain is this, "Create in me a clean heart and purify me, and purify me. Create in me a clean heart so I may worship thee". These words can help in getting rid of the useless clutter that we hold onto, the clutter in our hearts that blocks our ability to praise and worship God, the clutter that prevents spiritual freedom, spiritual joy.

May you find time to do some deep cleaning of your drawers and cupboards and may the process lead you deep into the corners of your heart where the real work begins. May you find your spirit dancing to the music you discover through deep cleaning.

Questions to ponder:
What do I harbor in the corners of my heart?
What jobs am I putting off?

I Should Know Better

❧

In the morning, O Lord, you hear my voice; in the morn-
ing I lay my requests before you and wait in expectation.
—PSALM 5:3

❧

Spring is coming to an end and the days of summer seem to be in full view. One evening I was considering the days of summer and finding them to be gone and they were not even here yet! Soon I was overwhelmed by the list of things already on my calendar. It was amazing to me how quickly I felt my muscles tense, my heart race, my mood sadden. I tried desperately to fall asleep, but my mind kept reeling over and over the discovery that my summer appears to be totally booked. Summer appeared to be gone as soon as I looked at it. I felt a slight sense of panic. I want to reflect with you about the topic of taking your own advice.

Here's some good advice. Take one day at a time and live it as though it were your last day here on this earth. This is the advice I often hear myself offer, when asked, to family, friends and individuals within the community who are waiting for things in their life to happen or who seem overwhelmed by a busy schedule. I recommend they take time daily for quiet activities, such as reading, listening to music, sitting in nature, etc., in order to balance their busy schedules. The practice of quieting oneself allows for the spirit to become fully active in guiding our lives. Yet if I know this and if I firmly believe that God guides my path on a daily basis helping me to make decisions along the way, shouldn't I know better than to get all stressed out over something I am only anticipating? Where is that good advice when I need it?

The words reeling in my head this particular evening soon turned to "you are not practicing what you preach!" Have you ever caught yourself in the midst of needing to take your own advice? If I have given this advice shouldn't it be a part of who I am? Shouldn't it come naturally? It doesn't. It is humbling to be in a situation where you do not have the answer (which is frequent for me) for it causes you to seek counsel, to cry out for help. That evening of sleeplessness was a reminder to me that I am not in control. It is only with God's guidance that I can live my life with a sense of peace and every time I fill my schedule with activities I think are important without first praying for God's counsel, without engaging the Holy Spirit, I am acting outside of my relationship with God. Peace turns to stress.

Returning to bed I prayed about the activities of the summer. I prayed for God to provide calm to my reeling head and told myself to trust him to direct me to the most important ones and for the ability to say no to activities not necessary in my life. I also remembered that the summer calendar, which seems daunting and far too structured for my liking is simply a tentative schedule of events. The world will continue in an unknown fashion and there are a million things that could change the level of priority for each of the items I have listed on my calendar.

As we strive to fulfill our purpose in life we need to reach out and accept advice, counsel, and guidance in our decision-making. Each of us will accomplish our purpose in a meaningful fashion if we believe these words found in Jeremiah 29:11, "For I know the plans I have for you," says the Lord. "They are plans for good and not for disaster, to give you a future and a hope." When we truly trust God to care for us and to be with us through every situation in life we allow our spirit to be alive and strong. As we stray from trusting and lean on our own finite understanding we risk damaging or squelching the very spirit that gives us direction.

The best advice we can receive comes from the Holy Spirit, which resides within us. We can seek advice or counsel from others in an effort to come to a conclusion, but if we fail to seek the guidance of the spirit we miss the most valuable insight available to us. The advice I share with others is not simply what I know it is what I feel, what I have experienced. It is God's advice.

Listening for guidance from the spirit living within brings peace. We are faced with so many opportunities, choices and activities for our lives. Yet, it is understandable that while we search for ways to incorporate all the activities we have come to enjoy into our lives something has to be given up. So, we reprioritize our lives.

As you prioritize your activities be sure to seek the counsel of the Holy Spirit and you will do so with a sense of acceptance for the activities you will be fortunate to participate in. Remember to take one day at a time and to live each day as though it were your last day on earth. That's good advice; I think I'll take it!

Questions to ponder:
When do I find my schedule too full?
How do I deal with overbooked calendars?
When do I balance my busy life with quiet activities?

Excuses, Excuses

꧂

I will instruct you and teach you in the way you should
go; I will counsel you and watch over you. —PSALM 32:8

꧂

"Oh my, what a busy summer I have ahead of me." Will I be tempted to use that excuse? The world is full of excuses. Blame is cast on almost anything you can think of. Personally, I am tired of excuses that people give as reasons for not caring for their own health. I am particularly frustrated when I catch myself making excuses. I have been caught! I want to share with you this month the topic of responsibility.

I realized this morning that I have made excuses about my own health habits three times in the last three days! Yikes! First of all, I told someone that I would like to do more biking if only I could find someone to bike with. I do not have a bicycle build for two. Next, I complained to myself after eating a delicious brownie at a graduation party that if only the wonderful cook who brought them would not have made them I would not have had to eat one. How crazy is that? My third catch came this morning when I in my selfishness felt like I did not want to get out of bed when I was nudged awake slightly earlier than I had planned to, even knowing from past experiences and heightened awareness that God nudges me awake earlier when he wants me to do something. I still rejected his call. Finally, I leapt out of bed as though I had been bitten and looked out the window to see that the sky in the west was very dark. The Lord knows how important it is for me to walk early in the morning before my day starts and he was trying to tell me that the rain was coming and if I did not want to get wet I had better get going.

I am grateful for people like you who read my reflections. Taking time to reflect regularly has allowed me to reflect deeply into my soul and identify areas in my heart that need work. And, yes, I see this is an area that needs work. So here I go, asking myself these questions and offering them to you as well.

How many of you have caught yourself making excuses for why you eat poorly, exercise irregularly, put off time for personal reflection, do not challenge your mind, or neglect a relationship? Be honest with yourself. You are human. I think it is fair to say that we all make excuses at times. The bottom line remains firm and that is that it is our own personal responsibility to take care of our body, mind, and spirit. The choice is ours.

Responsibility is all about choices and accepting the consequences that come with the choices we make. I am the only one that has to accept the extra calories I ingest, or getting caught in the rain when I am being lazy. No one else is responsible for my physical, mental or spiritual health. Excuses make us feel as though it is someone else's fault, but excuses lead to self-induced neglect.

There are many tools available to us that encourage positive health behaviors. Health clubs, seminars, books, and the Internet are loaded with health tips. The church offers bible studies, work groups and missions for strengthening our spirit. Doctors, nurses, clergy, parents, teachers, relatives and friends can support us in our venture to achieve maximum health, but they are not responsible for our health or lack of health. Each of us has this responsibility.

The "I am too busy" excuse is a big one during the summer. While some of you might assume that summer is a naturally healthy season I would just like to mention some of the possible contradictions to that belief. Although the weather is generally more conducive to physical activity, many of us may spend more time stooped over in the garden than doing cardiovascular activity such as walking or biking. Vacations generally mean sitting in a car or airplane for long periods of time. Attending graduations and weddings also involve sitting, and they have the added temptation of delicious food. These busy summer schedules often lead us to believe we can take a vacation from our church community or spiritual activities.

There are potential health risks that come with the active summer, back strain from gardening, deep vein thrombosis from long stretches of sitting in the car, and spiritual strain from lack of spiritual practice during the summer months. Spiritual strain is perhaps more subtle to our awareness. Symptoms may be less obvious. You may find yourself becoming more irritable, fatigued, resentful, depressed, or you may have difficulty focusing on your work. Your spirit needs constant refreshment. Daily refreshment.

If you are using the "I'm just too busy" excuse, your health will suffer. I encourage you to be honest with yourself as you evaluate whether you use excuses for not improving your health and to remember that you have choices to make. The responsibility is yours and only you will have to deal with the benefits or consequences that come with the choices you make. Dear Lord, Divine Physician, Heavenly Father, provide us each with your guidance as we make healthy choices for living.

Questions to ponder:
What is my favorite excuse?
What consequences have I experienced as a result of
neglecting healthy habits?

The Other Side of the Bed

✖✖

Therefore do not worry about tomorrow, for tomorrow
will worry about itself. Each day has enough trouble of
its own. —*MATTHEW 6:34*

✖✖

Nurses spend much of their time at the bedside and as a nurse I have been privileged to be at the bedside of many patients. On occasion I have been given the opportunity to learn from the other side of the bed. God does send me writing material in mysterious ways! Let this be my topic for reflection that you might pause and reflect as well.

Over the years I think we all have experiences of illness that come out of nowhere and we are suddenly in a situation we were not prepared for. As I wondered what was going on in my body and why did I suddenly need to be in bed accepting care from others, I also wondered if there was a deeper meaning to this time of being on the other side of the bed. All of my life I have believed there is a purpose for everything I have encountered. Usually I discovered the meaning long after the event and then reflected on it. I am now a little quicker to reflect.

What could be learned from my physical state, from needing to be in the hospital? Plenty. For starters, I think it is very funny that we are "patients" when we are in the bed and for me anyway not the least bit "patient" with being there. Perhaps it is through being there that we learn patience and then become patient. I will say that as the days passed I did become patient with the process because I had no other alternative. God was and is in control and all of the healthcare providers were using their gifts and talents to make me well and the process could not be rushed.

A new level of empathy presented itself from the other side of the bed. I try to put myself in the patient's shoes when I work with them, keeping their response to a situation in mind without inflecting my own response. I may not always do this very well, but it is what I strive to do. What I discovered is that it is very hard as a patient to help those caring for you to understand all the intricate pieces of life that are affected by an illness. So I learned that when I am empathetic with another I am only empathetic to the degree I see the situation as affecting the person. There is always much I do not know about the person in the bed. Nor will I, or should I need to know everything about them. What is important is that I remember there are layers of life and experience that affect people without my awareness and I must be conscious of acknowledging my inability to fully understand the way they feel.

Here is something else that kept coming to me as I experienced the other side of the bed. God commands us to "love your neighbor as yourself", Mark 12:31. Does this simply mean to be nice to your neighbor as you are nice to yourself, or does it mean that I should take a deeper look at the way I care for myself. Have I become so focused on caring for others that I have neglected some important self-care? Tough question. One which I was quick to answer with a firm, 'well, of course not'. But further reflection revealed more questions than answers. Perhaps I do neglect part of my own well-being in an effort to serve others. The truth is I love to care for and serve others much more than I do myself. I felt it less important even thought it selfish to consider my personal needs before others. Honestly, even after days of reflecting on this point, I am still struggling with this lesson to some extent. The reality is I cannot love and care for others if I do not love and care enough for myself to maintain a strong physical, emotional and spiritual state of being. So what does that mean? Do I have to quit what I am doing? Definitely not! I simply need to step back and honor my personal needs so that I can be better prepared to love and care for others.

Here is the next lesson learned from the other side of the bed. I must allow others to care for me. To this I struggle, it is hard to let others do things for me. Yet, when I think about the peace and joy I feel when I am able to help someone else how can I prevent others from experiencing this feeling. This is self-ishness on my part. This is ego. This is a damaging state to be in. I must allow others to show their love for me as I enjoy showing my love to those in need.

It is my prayer that you will not have to learn lessons from the other side of the bed, although there is much to be learned there. Ponder if you will over the lessons I have learned. Being a patient does produce patience, empathy can only begin to understand what someone is going through, you must love and care for yourself then model that practice toward others, and finally allow others to love you the way you love them. Be cared for sometimes.

Questions to ponder:
What have I learned from a sick bed?
How do I let others care for me?
When have I felt the power of prayer?

Begin Again

❧

Finish each day and be done with it... You have done
what you could; some blunders and absurdities no doubt
crept in; forget them as soon as you can. Tomorrow is a
new day; you shall begin it well and serenely.
—RALPH WALDO EMERSON

❧

It is a beautiful summer morning and I am about to start my day.
Where do I start? Perhaps I will start with this job, no this one,
well perhaps yet this one. Finally settling into a small task before
going into the office, I relearn a valuable lesson. I am reminded
of God's infinite love for each of us and his unending patience
with us as we learn life lessons.

The project, which I had settled on, was a project I intended
to give as a gift. I have been slowly working at it and quite frankly
have been somewhat discouraged with my struggle to become
proficient at it. I continued to forge forward, however, believing
that good things are accomplished through determination and
commitment. Here is where the lesson comes in. After having
completed a portion of the project, and feeling that although
it was not perfect it was turning out to be pretty, I discovered
a hole, an irreparable hole. At first I was extremely frustrated.
Ready to give up. Ready to throw the project into the garbage
and never attempt it again. Quietly, a gentle whisper came to me
saying, "begin again", "begin again". God gives us the opportunity to begin again!

God's unfailing love never tires of our mistakes. We learn
from our mistakes. My desire to accomplish a task, which typically takes days, weeks or months in a shorter amount of time,

than is usually required, was like trying to take shortcuts in life. Generally, shortcuts lose the flavor of time, the beauty of sacrifice, the virtue of patience. When I got caught up in trying to accomplish the project too quickly I was depriving myself of the full experience in the process of creating a special gift.

This whisper to begin again, in such a soft gentle tone, prompted me to think about the many opportunities in life in which we may fail to accomplish goals, meet needs or give well deserved praise. This concept can be applied to areas of our health, as well. Sometimes we fail to take care of our bodies. We pretend we do not need to exercise or eat well. Only to discover that we have a lot of catching up to do in order to get ourselves back to a good physical state. We must begin again. There are times when we allow ourselves to believe that what we read or see on television will have no influence on us and that we do not need to be diligent about screening what we allow into our minds. Fear, anxiety, physical illness can result from misleading messages. Our diligence must begin again.

Spiritually, we can look at ourselves and begin to believe that we are hopeless, not good enough, that we are worthless. We can become broken and afraid to try new things or even to finish old things. This message, begin again, reminds us that God sees us differently than the world does. God has total faith in us and offers us his guidance in our lives. We need only to call on his strength to be able to begin again. We must remember when we fall into bad habits, or poor choices in life, that we can begin again. When we are unfaithful to our commitments, we can begin again. When we are uncaring toward others, we can begin again.

In Psalm 86:1-7 we read, "Bend down, O Lord, and hear my prayer; answer me, for I need your help. Protect me, for I am devoted to you. Save me, for I serve you and trust you. You are my God. Be merciful, O Lord, for I am calling on you constantly.

Give me happiness, O Lord, for my life depends on you. O Lord, you are so good, so ready to forgive, so full of unfailing love for all who ask your aid. Listen closely to my prayer, O Lord; hear my urgent cry. I will call to you whenever trouble strikes, and you will answer me." What a beautiful message this is for us to hold on to. Always ready to be there for us. What an amazing thought. It is difficult to remember at times that we are always forgiven and capable of starting over in all situations in our life.

When I am in my car, unfortunately my radio at home does not pick up the signal; I always listen to WNWC Christian radio. There is a song that is played frequently by a group called *Casting Crowns*, from a CD of the same title. The song is, <u>Who Am I</u>, and I would encourage you to listen for it on the radio or pick up this CD. In the song there is a message about God's ability to look at individual sin and care enough to watch us rise again. Please try to locate this song; I do not want to mix up the lyrics for you as they have been so perfectly written.

What I find to be even more amazing is the way God uses everyday occurrences to remind me of his constant presence and unfailing love in my life. When I am frustrated by my inability to learn new skills or master old ones I am reminded that I must not give up because God is not giving up on me. He is asking me with a soft, gentle whisper to BEGIN AGAIN.

Questions to ponder:
When have I given up on a project?
Was I rushing through the steps?
How can I become more patient with the process?

CHAPTER 5

Hope and Trust

The Divine Weaver

My life is but a weaving between the Lord and me
I know not of the colors he weaveth steadily
Sometimes he weaveth sorrow and I in foolish pride
Forget he sees the upper and I the underside
Not until the loom is silent and the shuttle ceases to fly
Will God unveil the canvas and reveal the reason why
The dark threads were as needful in the weaver's skillful hand
As the threads of gold and silver in the pattern that he's planned.
AUTHOR UNKNOWN

Just Wait

~~

I say to myself, "The Lord is my portion; therefore I will wait for him." The Lord is good to those whose hope is in him, to the one who seeks him; it is good to wait quietly for the salvation of the Lord. —LAMENTATIONS 3:24-26

~~

I waited and I waited and I waited for a message to write to you about. The 18th of the month was my deadline for writing this reflection letter. Trusting God would send me a message, I waited. Then on the 18th of the month, at 5:00 a.m., I was awakened with the topic for my reflection circling through my head. The topic is *waiting*. Sometimes I do not pick up the on hints God sends me very well I guess, I smiled to myself when I thought about several people I had told that I was *waiting* for God to send me a topic for discussion. What a gracious God. My trust in God and his belief in me allowed me to hear his message and then be stirred enough to get out of bed and write it down.

What does it mean to wait? What do we do while we wait? What can waiting offer us? We hear so many statements with this word in it like, "good things come to those who *wait*", "you will just have to *wait* for it, "just *wait* until your father gets home", and "anything worth having is worth *waiting* for". I am sure you recognize some of these statements. I can bet many of you have used one or two of these statements. But what do they really mean for us?

The dictionary defines the word *wait* this way, "to remain in a place or in a state of inactivity, indecision, delay, or anticipation because of some event expected to happen or a person expected to arrive, to be in readiness, to be set aside for a later action, to remain undone for the time being". It goes on to define *to wait out* as "to endure something distressing for instance a storm or a setback, by hoping that it will change for the better". Waiting has become easier for me over the years, yet there are still times when waiting causes some anxiety. Just because it has become easier does not mean I am always good at it. If I have a project in the house that I want to have done I usually want it done yesterday rather than waiting until next week. When I need to have my hair done I generally like to have it done that day, I do not like to wait for an appointment. There is a sense of urgency to my needs. Have you ever had these feelings?

We do not wait for very much in this world. The Internet has us connected to resources we used to wait days for by mail. When I think about it I used to be pretty excited about the travel maps and guides that would come in the mail when we were planning a vacation. I cannot say I get the same level of enthusiasm from sitting at the computer with Map quest. We have options for fast food, but consider the level of anticipation and excitement you have when you sit down to a thanksgiving dinner that took hours to prepare. I see a pattern building. There is more joy and satisfaction when there has been anticipation, planning and waiting.

What do we do while we wait? Many people become anxious. They fidget. They stew. They are impatient and often become angry. These responses to waiting cause increased stress on the body, mind and spirit. They lead to sleeplessness, nausea, headaches, harsh words that can damage relationships, and feelings of loss of control. As we learn to appreciate our opportunities to wait we develop patience and gain peace in our heart. What I do when I am waiting is pray. I decided long ago that I would pray while I was waiting. Whether waiting in line at the grocery store, waiting at a stoplight, or waiting to fall asleep I offer up prayer for whatever comes into my mind. I have decided that waiting times can be productive rather than destructive if I allow them to be. By the way I had been praying pretty intently as I waited for this message!

What can waiting offer us? I believe it can bring us great joy. Waiting offers us hope and we gain insight into life. It provides us with time for inner reflection and discovery. We can review the facts, understand the consequences and reap the fullest reward. We adjust and ready ourselves for what lies ahead in our lives. Unable to know the future we are encouraged when we wait on the Lord, putting our full trust in God to lead the way as we wait for the unfolding of our life. We ready ourselves for the road ahead. If we make ourselves ready to travel the road ahead we can appreciate more fully the path along the way. Waiting offers us time to prepare for the next minutes, days and years of life as they unfold.

Sometimes we are impatient with the way our life is creeping along. Perhaps we want to be finished with school, to advance in our job, or to making a move across the country, but we are still waiting. Have you ever noticed that waiting can teach you to become patient? Think of the patience God has with you and me. God is waiting for us to turn to him in our struggles, with our fears, and in celebration of our triumphs. God is a patient and loving God. He will wait forever for us to come to him.

Each year with the anticipation of spring we find ourselves in hopeful waiting of the opportunity for refreshing our souls with newness of life. It is a time of deep reflection, renewal and waiting. We wait for the most glorious event our lives, the promise of eternal life. We celebrate in hope of our own resurrection and the opportunity to meet our savior face to face. What an awesome thought. Well worth the WAIT.

Questions to ponder:
What am I waiting for in life?
How has God been faithful to my waiting?
What has been the greatest experience I have had that involved waiting?

I Told You So

༺༝

May your unfailing love rest upon us, O Lord, even as we put our hope in you. —PSALM 33:22

༺༝

It is official. Winter is over. Do you ever wonder if God is thinking, I told you so? Every year we witness the changing of the seasons, but don't we sometimes question whether the change will really happen? There are rich messages for trusting God in the changing of the seasons. So, too, are the changing seasons of our lives filled with messages about trusting God. Let me offer for reflection the topic of trusting God and the ever famous statement, I told you so.

Has anyone ever asked you for your advice, your opinion, or your direction? After you shared your wisdom with them have they ever disregarded it as though they did not trust you? Have you ever wanted to say, I told you so, when things work out the way you had suggested in the first place? Have you ever wanted to say, I told you so, when they come to you disappointed that they had not trusted your wisdom, your judgment, your direction in the first place? Do you suppose God would like to say, I told you so, when we have failed to trust his wisdom, his judgment, his direction?

I imagine he would, but like any good parent or friend knows it is simply something you do not say. Rather you wait, as God does, patiently for the development of a trusting relationship, for the relationship to solidify. In this long wait for winters end I found myself trusting God's timing would be perfect in answering a prayer for my children. As the deadline for an answer drew near I began to doubt what I knew to be true. God would provide the details in perfect timing I kept telling myself, but doubt and fear crept into my mind. What would happen if the plan fell through? What if things did not work out? Where was my trust going?

I began to consider the bigger picture in the story that was unfolding. Isn't it true that some of the best stories in our lives have a suspenseful chapter or two, which allows God's goodness to shine in the final chapter? Exemplifying the power of God's never failing love? You know a chapter that ends with sort of an, I told you so flair? This kind of ending reminds us how important it is to totally trust God's power in supporting us in whatever situation we find ourselves in.

I pondered this suspense chapter. I wondered if the suspense chapter is filled with the evil of Satan's presence. I wonder if these chapters are a time where God trusts us to hold onto his promises for our life while Satan temps us with doubt and fear. Screaming in our ear all the evil that could happen, telling us God does not love us or care about us, suggesting that if God loved us he would not allow us to experience struggles or scary times in our life. I believe perhaps our times of doubt and fear are indeed caused by the loud voice of evil.

Beyond the loud voice of evil, however, is the gentle, patient whisper of God that called out to me during this time of doubt and fear and asked me again to trust in him beyond my own understanding. In Proverbs 3:5-6 we read, "Trust in the Lord with all your heart and lean not on your own understanding; in all your ways acknowledge him, and he will make you paths straight". In quieting myself enough to hear the gentle whisper of God's love I will strengthen my spirit to do battle against evil thoughts.

I am not sure about you, but I am grateful that God does not say, I told you so every time this child of his doubts his infinite wisdom. He is a patient, gracious God and I am a child continuing to solidify my relationship with him through quiet moments set aside to listen to the voice of God. May your battles with the loud voice of evil be fought by listening for the whisper of God saying trust in me rather than I told you so.

Questions to ponder:
Where do I need to trust God in my life?
How will I make time to listen to God's whisper above the evil chatter?

The Right Road

God isn't going to let you see the distant scene. So you might as well quit looking for it. He promises a lamp unto our feet, not a crystal ball into the future. We do not need to know what will happen tomorrow. We only need to know he leads. MAX LUCADO

Ah, summer! A time for traveling to see loved ones. One summer day, in an effort to save travel time, I took a new road to my destination (this was before GPS). So I reviewed the map and calculated the timing and off I went. It was interesting to me that although I clearly knew it would take the same amount of time and that I was indeed heading north as my compass indicated I felt uncomfortable in this new territory. Stopping to review the map, I could not help but question, was I on the right road? I was prompted to reflect on the topic of being on the right road.

As you travel through life do you ever feel like you are on the wrong road? The territory is new, unfamiliar. You have stepped out of your comfort zone. Perhaps you are heading to a new destination uncertain of what you might find when you arrive. You are hopeful that it will be all you dreamed it would be. There is a level of concern as you move ahead through unfamiliar territory. Will you get there in time? Will the road be rough ahead? Will you have enough energy (gas so to speak) to make the journey?

The message that kept coming to me as I traveled this unknown road was this, trust in me to lead you. Trust in me to lead you. The reason I started out on this adventure was because I had felt God was leading me to make this trip. So, why did I now doubt the path I was taking? As I stopped to review the map I discovered that indeed I was on the exact road I was supposed to be on to travel from point A to point B. Clearly, there was no need to worry.

Well up ahead there was major construction, which I was sure would cause a serious delay in my arrival time, my anticipated arrival time. Ultimately, I was there in plenty of time. It was just not my time line. Once again, *God's time* was the calming response I received to my questions. Why is the traffic going so slowly? Why can't I get there faster? *God's time.* I used my travel day to receive and reflect on an important message. Trust that you will be lead on the right road, meeting and overcoming road blocks to arrive at your destination for the purpose of your life in *God's time.*

I slept well knowing I had been reminded of a valid truth. God is always in control. He will keep me on the right road. I chuckled to myself as I traveled home and encountered yet additional concerns about being on the right road. Evidently, there was a deeper message I had not picked up the day before. This time I had accessed the Internet for assistance in finding the back roads that would take me home. Well, let me say this, regardless of the correctness or incorrectness of the directions I had time to pick up a strong message during my additional driving time. The message was this. The journey will take as long as it will take! There was nothing I was going to do to shorten my return home having steered myself in the direction I was traveling. Likewise, my life journey will proceed at the pace it is suppose to so there is no need to try to speed it up.

How often do we rush our lives? How often do we wish our circumstances would resolve only to discover we are unable to hurry the process? There are times when we cannot alter our journey. We can however, learn to appreciate the journey for all the wisdom, beauty, and experience it provides. Once again, trusting God to provide what I needed in this adventure was a comfort. I grew to appreciate this journey during my extra time on the road.

Now, I could have panicked, fretted about being an hour and 10 minutes late (for my time frame), blamed the Internet for my troubled travel plans, but I didn't. I had learned my lesson the previous day that God would be in charge of my timing for returning home. I only needed to focus on what message was available to me in this experience. The journey will take as long as the journey will take regardless of the detours, smooth sailing on open roads, rough roads or traffic I might encounter. My life circumstances will progress in a similar fashion to my travel experience.

Your life is progressing at the speed in which it is suppose to progress. The ability to appreciate the journey as a process and not only a means to a final destination is so important for your well-being. We can find peace in knowing that God will lead us on the right road at a pace fitting God's timing, which will ultimately be the right road for us and will lead us to destination and purpose he has planned.

Questions to ponder:
Have I ever felt lost?
How did I gain my sense of direction?
How can I trust my arrival to my purpose in life is all in God's timing?

Spinning Out of Control

℔℔

God isn't going to let you see the distant scene. So you might as well quit looking for it. He promises a lamp unto our feet, not a crystal ball into the future. We do not need to know what will happen tomorrow. We only need to know he leads. —MAX LUCADO

℔℔

There is something about September that has always been appealing to me. As I walked one August morning I found myself longing for September. What was it about the beginning of fall that I longed for that morning? It was the end of the spinning, a new beginning, an opportunity for centering. I wish to share with you a reflection on the topic of spinning out of control.

As I walked I thought about the last weeks of summer filled with activity, almost frantically packing in one activity after another just to get it all in before summers end. It seemed as though the days were beginning to fly by faster and faster before my eyes. I suddenly remembered having a top as a child and it occurred to me that life is very much like a top in a number of ways. Perhaps the familiarity with this childhood toy is the reason God prompted me to use it as an example of the message being sent.

The top I had growing up was very colorful and intricately detailed. When held upright and gently twirled you could still identify the colors as it spun before your eyes. However, when the top was encouraged to spin faster and faster the colors began to run together and even became dull almost negligible. There was certainly no chance of identifying any true color or design when the top was spinning that hard. The faster the top spun the more out of control it became, slipping away from the hand that was spinning it. For a while once released the top would stand upright and almost dance across the floor. Eventually, though it would begin to wobble, clatter to the floor and stop.

Is this perhaps what happens to our spirit when we are encouraged by this world to spin faster and faster? Take on one more task, complete one more job, see one more sight, make a little more money, do, do, do. Soon we are spinning so fast we begin to pull away from the one keeping us centered and stable. We break away and spin on our own further and further away from our source of strength.

I believe that the colors and design of my spirit are brighter when I spin under the guidance of my creator. It is my hope that others can see this true spirit. Unfortunately, I know all too well that I am guilty of coming dangerously close to spinning out of control and I know it is then that my true spirit is dulled. It is blurred by the rapid pace I get myself into. In those last weeks of August I found myself spinning away from my center and quickly beginning to topple over and bump against the floor. By allowing myself to stop and be centered once again I hope to recover the color of my true spirit back into view.

When we allow ourselves to become disconnected from our source of strength, when we lose our connection to the one who spins our world gracefully, we struggle to keep ourselves upright and maintain the vibrancy of our spirit.

September has always been the time of the year when I stop and think about how fast I was beginning to spin. How dangerously close I was coming to letting go and spinning out of control. I think for many people September is a time to take a deep breath and slow down after the rapid pace of summer. It is a time of routine rebuilding. So often our spiritual activities are disrupted during the summer months due to vacations, guests, projects. It is good to recapture spiritual practices.

Fall is a time of settling down. It seems a natural time to slow the spinning world and maintain balance under the guiding hand of the Father. When you are centered the color of your true spirit is visible to the world. Let your life spin at a speed that allows us to see the color of your true spirit.

Questions to ponder:
What is my favorite season for slowing down?
What is the color of my spirit?

What's Good About It?

And the Holy Spirit helps us in our distress. For we don't even know what we should pray for, nor how we should pray. But the Holy Spirit prays for us with groanings that cannot be expressed in words. And the Father who knows all hearts knows what the Spirit is saying, for the Spirit pleads for us believers in harmony with God's own will. And we know that God causes everything to work to-gether for the good of those who love God and are called according to his purpose for them.

ROMANS 8:26-28

Well the actual temperature is –19 and the wind chill is – 40 so as I exit the bed to greet the morning I wonder to myself, what's good about it, before I utter those words, Good Morning! Beyond being a great conversation starter this morning's weather has prompted a topic for reflection. Let's take some time to consider what's good about *it*, whatever *it* might be.

This frigid morning while I am searching for the good in it, it occurs to me that God's faithfulness is exhibited in each sunrise. God's faithfulness is evident in the sunset at the close of each day. Therefore, there must then be something good behind every difficulty we face or God would give up on creating a new day, a new opportunity for each of us.

Have you ever been blindsided by a piece of information you were oblivious to? Perhaps something happens that you would never have imagined happening? Maybe you discover that someone has kept a secret from you and it hurts as you learn the details or a family member has acted in a way that embarrasses you. Have you ever wondered what good will ever come from *it*?

Although your initial response to unwanted news might be to question God's presence at all, to blame someone or something for the circumstances, or to question, how could this happen, I believe it is important to first search out what is good about the situation or it will quickly grow into something it is not. We must maintain a balanced perspective and consider potential options before we jump to conclusions or we will find ourselves in a pit of doom.

In this world there is often more focus on what is wrong or bad about any given situation than what is good. For instance, the media is excellent at bombarding us with negative news. They will inform us again and again about the wind chill being 40 below without a mention of the bright sunshine. Granted it is important for us to know we should bundle up when we go outside, but in Wisconsin that should be a given. My spirit cries, 'Forget the gloom and doom. Tell me about the good stuff'.

So I always try to ask myself, what is good about it? I believe there is something good that will come out of every situation, that God will bring all things into good. My spirit, your spirit, longs to know the good in others, in our circumstances, in ourselves and that spirit dwells within us to protect us from the brokenness of evil. The spirit is there to heal the heart in difficult times.

Recently, I had a conversation with a friend of mine who had seen a program on TV predicting the end of the world. It cited evidence from both the Mayan tribe and ancient China, which predicts the world will end on a certain date. What would be good about that? Actually, for those of us who believe in eternal life, the good could be that there would no longer be any pain or suffering and there would be an end to all evil. Certainly, it takes a well-rested spirit and a healthy relationship with

God to support the weight of gloom and doom and to be able to identify, what's good about *it*. My spirit is much better equipped to identify good when it is rested and when I have taken time to nurture my relationship with God.

I encourage you to rest your spirit, protect it from the constant negativity portrayed in the media or in neighborhood gossip. Read an inspirational book. Listen to music. Laugh over lunch. Daydream. These simple activities will strengthen your spirit to be ready to identify the good when someone asks you, what's good about *it*?

Questions to ponder:
How do I start my day? With negative news? With a brisk walk in nature?
In what simple ways can I nurture my spirit into restfulness to manage the strain of daily life in our world?
What would I do differently today if I knew the world would end tomorrow? If we do not know, why wait?

The Correctly Arranged Path

⁓

So I go on, not knowing, I would not, if I might, I would
rather walk in the dark with God than go alone
in the light; I would rather walk with Him
by faith than walk alone by sight.
—MARY GARDINER BRAINARD

⁓

Can you believe how fast the time is going? Are you doing everything you want to do? Everything you are supposed to do? How do discern which activities are right for you and your family? What if you choose the wrong activity? These questions can weigh heavy on your mind. So, I want to reflect with you on the topic of journeying along the correctly arranged path.

One summer I had the opportunity to walk a labyrinth at St. Anthony's Retreat Center in Marathon, WI. In doing so, I was struck by the similarity between the labyrinth and a God guided life. For those of you who have never seen a labyrinth you might wonder, what is a labyrinth? Good question. Until a few years prior to my visit to the retreat center I had no idea what a labyrinth was. I have become so enamored with them that I convinced my husband to create one for me in our backyard. I enjoy it immensely. A labyrinth is a walking spiritual growth or meditation tool. It looks like a maze at first; however, it is not a maze in that it has no roadblocks or dead ends. The labyrinth leads you on an unobstructed journey into the center and then back. It is a metaphor for journeying into the center of your being and then returning to the world.

The labyrinth is an ancient symbol appearing in areas all around the world. Perhaps the most well known labyrinth is in the floor of the Cathedral of Notre Dame Chartres just outside of Paris. It is 800 years old. Briefly, my understanding is that the labyrinth was created during a time when it was too dangerous to make a spiritual pilgrimage. The labyrinth symbolized the pilgrimage and afforded safety for those who walked it (a very brief history, please look it up online. There is lots of information out there).

Anyway, back to my reflection. As I walked the labyrinth, which was simply cut into the grass, I found myself initially trying to look ahead to see where I was going. I also found myself hesitating as to whether I was on the right track and being afraid I would make a wrong turn. However, shortly after I began the journey a peaceful feeling came over me and I found myself relaxing into the rhythm of the walk, the journey. I began to trust that even through the twists and turns of the labyrinth, like the twists and turns of life I would be led safely to my personal destination. I was able to drop the worry about which way I should go and reflect on the connection being made to the importance of God's guidance in my life. Like the labyrinth God has created a journey for me and if I trust in his guidance I will arrive at the center of my being fully connected to his purpose for my life.

The journey also brought to mind Proverbs 3:5, "Trust in the Lord with all your heart and lean not on your own understanding; in all your ways acknowledge him, and he will make your paths straight". To "trust in the Lord with all your heart" means to put away reservation. This is not always easy for me. The monster of fear often distracts me. Fear has reared its ugly head and prompted me to question the timing, the journey, or the motivation for activities and decisions I unexpectedly face.

It is then I must remember to "lean not on your (my) own understanding" because it is impossible for me to fully understand what the Lord has planned for me. I must simply trust in his guidance of my life journey. By acknowledging that God is in control of my life God will ensure that my path is made "straight".

As I entered the labyrinth at the retreat center there was no "straight" path that is if you consider the definition of straight as being the shortest distance between two points. But, if you consider the definition of straight as being "correctly arranged", it makes perfect sense. My life journey, your life journey may not be the most direct path between two points, it may have twists and turns, but undoubtedly we will arrive at the appropriate destination.

The questions that fill our minds regarding decisions we make for the future are less confining, troubling and weighty when we believe in God's unfailing love and concern for our well-being. So like entering a labyrinth for the purpose of spiritual reflection about the journey life is taking you on, Proverbs 3:5 reminds us that as we trust in the Lord completely without reservation about the direction we are headed, having consulted God and acknowledged that he is in control, we will be lead down the "correctly arranged" path toward accomplishing the purpose God has set forth for each of us.

Questions to ponder:
How often do I lean on my own understanding?
How often do I trust and lean on God?
Can I acknowledge a correctly arranged path for my life?

CHAPTER 6

Making Connections
ઌઌ

"I was on a train on a rainy day. The train was slowing down to pull into a station. For some reason I became intent on watching the raindrops on the window. Two separate drops, pushed by the wind, merged into one for a moment and then divided again – each carrying with it a part of the other. Simply by that momentary touching, neither was what it had been before. And as each one went on to touch other raindrops; it shared not only itself, but what it had gleaned from the other. I saw this metaphor many years ago and it is one of my most vivid memories. I realized then that we never touch people so lightly that we do not leave a trace. Our state of being matters to those around us."
—*PEGGY TABOR MILLIN*

Personal Connections

૱૱

Staying connected is easier than ever. Is it?

૱૱

Today as I searched the web for information relating to a health promotion topic I felt very frustrated. The underlying cause of my frustration was not that I could not understand the technology (yet I admit I am far from expert), but rather that I was unable to make a connection. I found myself feeling more frustrated with each page-down activity. There was one screen after another of questions to answer, followed by a statement suggesting that I must first complete a different form before I completed the current one. It would have been helpful if they would have mentioned that prior to my investing 20 minutes toward the completion of the questions. My frustration was growing. What was my blood pressure doing? I felt guilty for having wasted 20 minutes of my day and, I felt alone! I need to talk about making personal connections.

We can dial-up, log-on, e-mail, forward, browse, instant message, chat, text, twitter, tweet, but can we connect? Do you connect? I am not referring to the ability to download volumes of material. I am asking you to consider whether you make connections. Computers, as well as other technological tools have a purpose. They are good for society in many ways. My concern is that they may also prove to be unhealthy to your body, mind and spirit.

Using my example, consider how different it could have been for me to obtain health promotional materials had I been able to talk to a real live flesh and blood person. They could have directed me to access their website, yes, but they might also have been able to explain to me that there were certain steps to take to achieve the end goal more quickly. I believe that I would have felt calmer, less guilty and less alone having made a connection with someone. Even if it would have taken me 20 minutes!

People need people. We need each other. We are called to take care of one another, carry each other's burdens, and support those in need. Can we do that and still utilize the technology of today? I believe we can. Computers and medical technology can save time and save lives in some situations. However, computers, as well as medical technology can become burdensome at times. I believe that computers can destroy families, marriages, personal health, values and self-esteem when they become our sole source of communication. There is an abundance of helpful information to be found on the Internet and mixed into that information is an abundance of destructive information.

Computerized phone systems can be challenging. How many of you enjoy making a call to a business intending to ask a question about your bill only to be greeted by a stream of options that do not seem to cover your question? If you press one, or two you might get another set of numbers to press. With hope you forge forward and press yet another number and hear a recording that does not begin to answer your question. Yet, there is never a human being on the other end to ask. I wonder how many people give up or decide not to bother calling about their concerns, because they know they will have to play this game? I wonder how many people feel alone about their health concerns because they do not know which choice will provide them with the answers they are looking for.

How often is the computer on in your home? How much time do you spend having conversations with family members about world events, local events, hopes, and dreams, God? Is there a balance or is the scale tipped away from personal contact. Will we soon lose our uniqueness because we are fed information so mechanically that we fail to consider what this information means for our life? Isolation can exist under these circumstances. Isolation often leads to depression, hopelessness, and helplessness. Furthermore, let's consider all the physical risks associated with computer time, eye strain, neck strain, carpal tunnel syndrome, back strain, weight gain.

The risk of cutting off personal connections altogether is most troublesome to me. We can pay our bills, balance our checkbooks, order our clothes, groceries, send notes, and never have to talk to a single person. Convenient, perhaps. Good? I don't think so.

If we are called to care for one another, how are we doing that via technology? Yes, we can treat medical symptoms, we can provide health information, but can we truly care for the individual? I believe I see the face of God in those I meet. I enjoy looking into someone's eyes and seeing their spirit. How do you feel when someone smiles at you when you are having a bad day? I feel lifted up when someone smiles at me particularly when I am having a bad day. Often, you can tell when you are talking to someone on the phone whether they are happy or sad by the sound of their voice. You might comment to them about what you hear and be the lift they need in their day. I cannot see the face of God in the computer, or hear the voice of God in a recording. God uses people to provide true spiritual enrichment for each of us.

Can we act toward the stranger in the way that God calls us to via technology? Perhaps in some ways. Yet, I believe in order to strengthen our spirits and grow spiritually we need to make personal connections. All the knowledge in the world cannot begin to affect someone's life the way a smile, kind word, gentle touch or listening ear can.

Questions to ponder:
What do I miss most in making personal connections?
What does it mean for my life if I do not miss the personal connections?

A Message Worth Repeating

No one has ever seen God; but if we love one another,
God lives in us and his love is made complete in us. 1
—*JOHN 4:12*

Sometimes I repeat myself. Often, I tell one son the same thing twice and the other son does not get the message at all. Sometimes I am so excited about an event that I berate the details over and over to anyone who will listen without realizing that my audience is getting tired of the same old story. This is a message worth repeating.

I am grateful for the amount of traveling I have been able to do with my family over the years. When we travel we enjoy attending church services within those communities being visited. Occasionally, we have had a few re-acquaintances with clergy and topics. A few weeks ago I found myself reflecting on the fact that the point of the message being given from the same individual had stayed the same as the previous time we had heard him speak and it had been months ago. As I came to this awareness I noted that in fact as often as we had listened to him over the years I believe he always brought us to this same message. It is a message worth repeating. He began his message by using a different set of circumstances to grab my attention and then smoothly lead me to the key point he wanted to drive home once again. Even though the point of his message was the same it was presented in such a way as to make it fresh and new not old and boring. He was successful in capturing my attention to a repetitious message. He was able to once again drive home a message that bears repeating. Isn't it true that the most important

messages in life deserve repeating? Why is that? Are some messages harder to remember or hold on to?

His message was not new. It was a reminder of God's call for
us to love one another. It remains constant. Love one another.
This is a phrase we have all heard many, many times. And if we
were to admit it we have probably preached it to our children or
friends when they have been down on someone in their life. Yet,
it seems to me as though this is a phrase that is hard to remember for some people or in certain situations. Why? What makes
this command so hard to follow? Perhaps we question whether
this is truly God's message for each of us? Maybe we question
whether we are capable of being loved or of giving love?

This message is more than three simple words. It is a call
to action. It requires you to do something. A call to put your
money where your mouth is so to speak. Walk the talk. How do
you begin to act out this message, a message we hear over and
over again, a message that deserves to be heard as more than
simple words, a message to be heard as an action to be taken?

The answer I believe begins with adopting an attitude of
caring. We need to care about others. We must go beyond our
family circle or group of friends to include those who are alone,
hurting, frightened, confused. We are called to care about every
single person on this earth, even those being tempted by evil
and those who have fallen into evil. We know all too well it is
not easy to love everyone. Not everyone appears to be lovable.
Thankfully, Jesus set an example for us to follow. He loved everyone. Everyone was welcome in his presence.

We read in John 3:16, "For God so loved the world that
he gave His only begotten Son, that whoever believes in Him
should not perish but have everlasting life." "Whoever believes
in Him", whoever! That includes those people who drive you
crazy, those people who irritate you to the end, and those people

who are different than you. We are all equal in God's eyes. We are all worthy of love.

Every day we need to reflect on our ability to love one another the way Jesus did taking the time to seek forgiveness for the times we have not acted in a loving manner toward another human being, reviewing our current practice of accepting others into our neighborhoods, into our communities, adopting new practices for loving one another. We already know how to do this. Caring for others can come easily if we simply search our heart for what is needed. Acts of kindness like sending cards, letters, a meal, giving a phone call, sending an email, dropping by, or offering to help with chores are all welcome ways of loving one another. For others who pose a challenge for us to love we are called to pray for them and in doing so we are extending love to them.

In addition, taking the opportunity to check your heart for signs of darkness towards others is important. Each and every one of us is a child of God and each of us is filled with the Holy Spirit. Opening our hearts to see Christ in the face of everyone we meet is a step toward fulfilling God's command to love one another. When our own spirit is soiled, fogged in by misconceptions of importance we are unable to identify worth in others. Judgment sets in and whenever judgment sets into our hearts we block our ability to truly love others.

We can get lost in the daily rush of things (this message I pass along to you seemingly on a regular basis as much for my own benefit as yours) turning our thoughts inward noting our own needs and overlooking the needs of others. We must search our hearts, clear our hearts of judgment, see Christ in the faces of those we meet and reach out in acts of kindness and prayer toward our neighbors and our community in order to fulfill God's command to love one another. Let this message of loving one another be repeated in your mind and heart on a regular basis without tiring of hearing it. Look at it with a fresh start each time you hear it.

Questions to ponder:
What are the messages being repeated in my life?
How do they become new again?
What can I do to show love for others today?

Cut the Chatter

ୟୁ

He who guards his lips guards his life, but he who speaks rashly will come to ruin. —PROVERBS 13:3

ୟୁ

My husband and I were planning a vacation out west skiing. As our vacation approached I anxiously looked forward to the uninterrupted conversations we would have. No work distractions. No cold callers. No meetings or schedules. It is funny how things work out when we gather expectations into our head. Twenty-four hours into our travel I lost my voice. Gone. I had never experienced laryngitis to that extent before, but there it was I certainly had a serious case of it. To say the least I had to *cut the chatter*. Any utterance of a word or forming of a sound had to be done with great respect to limit any strain on my vocal chords. Thank you God for a great topic for reflection, *cut the chatter.*

My husband is actually the quiet type. He is not the kind of person who will talk your ear off. Imagine if you will the scenario, the silence was deafening at times. Now please don't get me wrong, I like silence, love it at times, but I was silent for 3 full days, my own silence was deafening to me. Some of you might think that would be heavenly to have someone in your family lose their voice. More than one man on the trip commented that way when my husband explained that I had laryngitis, "That might not be so bad", they'd smile (I would venture to say Keith probably did enjoy the silence, at least a little).

The first day was really difficult. Frustrating! The inability to share my feelings about the beauty around us, to explain what I needed or to ask him a question about anything was really tough. Then it occurred to me, God had given me an opportunity to see the way in which we often fill our lives with mindless chatter. In my inability to talk I was not able to fill the space in my relationship with a lot of mindless chatter.

Ultimately, Keith and I were able to communicate what needed to be expressed. We enjoyed the beauty of the morning and evening sky, prepared great meals together and relaxed in the silent presence of one another. I began to take notice of others around us, the way they were in relationship with one another.

I found it interesting to see people in the ski lodges sitting together, but talking on their cell phones instead of talking to each other. I do not think there was a couple or a group allowing themselves to simply be in the presence of one another without idle chatter on their cell phones. Honestly, I likely only experienced this perception because I could not talk or use my cell phone not even if I would have needed to. I smiled to myself at the absurdity of taking it along with me on the mountain, but I had.

In the absence of vocal chatter, my spirit was given the opportunity to speak up. I thought I heard my spirit most of the time. I did not realize until I lost my voice that I need to listen even more intently. I became sharply aware of my spirit's need to be expressed. I am most used to using words to do that, but without a voice I had to find other ways to express joy, pain, love, sorrow.

Believe me; I am delighted to have my voice returning. For those of you who know me I am sure this scenario was hard to imagine, but I now see it as a gift teaching me to listen more closely to my own spirit and to be attentive toward those with no voice. It has encouraged me to look more deeply for the ways they might be expressing their true spirit.

Through this experience I gained a new awareness of the value of the spoken word. By the 4th day, when my voice began to return, I selected and used my words sparingly remaining awed by the ability to communicate that which is necessary without giving way to the use of idle talk, appreciating the presence of the spiritual connection in my relationship. I want to encourage you to *cut the chatter* in your life, slow the idle talk, and identify with deep appreciation the spiritual connectedness in your relationships.

Questions to ponder:
When have I experienced difficulty communicating?
How often do I use my cell phone when I am with friends?
ow does technology interfere with spiritual connectedness in my life?

It's Not About the Food

෬

Let them give thanks to the Lord for his unfailing love
and his wonderful deeds for men, for he satisfies the
thirsty and fills the hungry with good things.
—PSALM 107:8-9

෬

Several weeks ago the weather prevented my husband from working on the job site. He was home doing paperwork and meeting with potential customers. I was scheduled to be in the office, so I asked him if I could take him to lunch. He thought for a minute and then said, "No, that's all right I will just eat up some of the leftovers". I smiled at him, shook my head and said, "But it's not about the food".

How many times have you asked someone to come for dinner, go to lunch, or stop for coffee and had them respond to you with a million reasons why they are unable to do so. Reasons like, 'Oh, I can't get away today, I am just so busy', 'I am really not very hungry today', or 'I planned to use up the leftovers tonight', are common responses I hear people give all the time. Let's think about the true meaning behind these invitations. Do you really think the food is the most important part of the invitation? I would venture to say, absolutely not! The invitation is about relationship.

What I was asking my husband for that day was an opportunity for us to spend a few bonus minutes together. He is rarely around over the lunch hour and our schedules do get extremely busy, just like everyone else's. I saw a window of opportunity to share time with him in the middle of the week, a time when we could talk about the day's activities as they were unfolding, laugh a little, or just be together. Over the years, we have both discovered how important it is to make time for building healthy relationships.

I use the lunch or dinner invitation to catch up with friends, colleagues, relatives and sometimes to get to know new people in the community. It gives us an opportunity to be in a relaxed atmosphere, separated from the pressures of the day. These times together encourage us to focus on personal celebrations, accomplishments, and challenges. I believe these openings in our schedules are provided by God to strengthen our relationships. They allow us time to open up lines of communication in the midst of the fast pace in which we find ourselves immersed.

When we dive into life with our focus only on how fast we can accomplish our goals, I believe we miss the real reason we are here in the first place. For me that reason is to build relationships with one another as God's family. By extending or agreeing to an invitation to share food with one another I think we are truly addressing the need to be in relationship. Time together is the best food for spiritual hunger.

Our bodies need nutritious food to function properly and to be healthy and strong. Our spirit requires nutritious food as well. Food for the spirit is spending time in relationship. Relationship with others, with nature, and with our loving God provides the nutritious spiritual food we require to maintain our spiritual health.

By the way, I remember we did go to lunch that day. I have no recollection of the food we ate, I imagine it was good, but the moments together were better. I suggest you remember that it is truly not about the food. Our loved ones no matter if they are the head of the household or the child can suggest these invitations for sharing a meal together to satisfy the spiritual hunger of relationship, and we must consider responding as if it is the only time we will be able to make this particular memory, for indeed it is.

Questions to ponder:
When have I passed up an opportunity to
feed a relationship?
What feeds my spiritual hunger?

Step One

༄༅

The first step is the most important one.

༄༅

I stood on the promise that God would soon send me a message, one that I could share with all of you and woke up to realize he has been sending me the message for a week now and I have been reluctant to take the first step in communicating it to all of you. I want to share with you some thoughts about step one.

We had returned from a vacation to Colorado. Upon return, I found myself feeling somewhat disconnected. I was eager to reconnect with family and friends. As I attempted to retrieve my emails my computer server was not functioning. There was some message about an error in the server, for which I had little understanding. I knew I would have to call my Internet support contact, but, oh, how I hated the thought of wading through the list of numbers in order to talk to a real person. So I delayed calling. My emails remained in limbo. My connections to my family and friends and returning to "the real world" remained hidden somewhere behind my dark computer screen, yet I was willing to put off calling the source I knew could help me.

Have you ever had a piece of equipment break down? The toaster does not seem to be toasting, the curling iron is not heating up, the computer monitor remains black. What is *step one* for determining the nature of the problem? Check the power source. Is the item plugged in? Is there a connection being made? Are the lines open for power to flow?

How does this relate to each of us and spiritual reflection? Here is the connection: sometimes we breakdown, become disconnected or remain dark in our thoughts. We need to take the first step to resolving the problem by checking our source of power. Are we plugged in? Are the lines open or has the connection been severed by fear, greed, complacency? Whether the task is making a call, jumping into the water, moving one step forward, whether it is forgiveness, acceptance, or acknowledgement, breaking the process down into steps to be taken one at a time reduces that paralyzed feeling, which can be overpowering. Step one; identify the source of power for the energy needed to complete the task.

In regard to my computer I knew I had to make the call. When I did reach a real person he asked if I had checked the connections. I was able to say I had, but there still seemed to be something preventing the power from getting through the lines. A technical problem existed complicating the power source. Sometimes I think we too quickly feel we can fix our problems on our own, but many times we need to make the call and check the power source. When things are not working out in our lives, when they seem cloudy or dark, we need to do a power check. We need to consider whether we are truly connected or simply plugged in.

Step one: check your power source. Ask, am I connected to my power source? Only after step one can you proceed to the additional steps it will take for you to live this life fully with hope, faith and love. Outside my kitchen window the sunrise splashes color across the sky and I am filled with awe. There it is, *Step one*: Know Your Power Source.

Questions to ponder:
What is my source of power?
How do I know this power source will continue to serve me?
Am I connected or simply plugged in?

Hospitality

࠴࠴

Do not forget to entertain strangers, for by so doing some
people have entertained angels without knowing it.
—HEBREWS 13:2

࠴࠴

One summer day I was sent a message about the importance of hospitality and it was sent through an interaction I had with a 5-year-old boy. This little boy knew more about hospitality than many people I know. This is a topic worth considering.

Children say the cutest things anyway, but what this little boy said made me aware of how often we do not receive this kind of hospitality in the world today. Let me share this story with you. I had been visiting a job site with my husband, a place he had worked before, so this little boy knew my husband, but he had never met me. His mother introduced me and he reached out his hand and said he wanted to show me something. He was inviting me into his world. His face lit up with excitement as we approached a pen with 3 new little pigs. He explained to me that they were his sister's pigs and told me all about how they thought his shoes were food to eat. Quickly, he climbed over the fence to demonstrate to me what he had just explained. He sat down in the straw and let these 3 little pigs nudge him and nibble at his shoes giggling joyfully. As we got ready to leave, I said good-bye and thanked him for showing me the pigs. He waved and called out after us, "it was nice to meet your wife"! I have been smiling for weeks since.

What did this little boy demonstrate about the importance of hospitality? He pointed out how much the spirit likes random acts of kindness and appreciation. His actions toward me were totally kind, accepting and even appreciative. When we are accepted and appreciated we feel good. Our spirit feels good. When we receive random acts of kindness our spirit feels like smiling, rejoicing, and showing gratitude in return.

How many of you have had interactions with others that were anything but kind, accepting and appreciative? There is an air of selfishness in society, and a false idea of expectation. There is an assumption that we deserve things and often expect to get what we want without considering the appropriate way to ask. Sometimes, we decide it is not our responsibility to assist those in need and avoid them hoping someone else will help them. Do we think that they do not notice they are being put off? Do you think they do not feel the lack of kindness, acceptance and appreciation? I believe their spirit is well aware of the lack of hospitality.

If we fail to extend hospitality to others we miss opportunities to meet new people. We miss opportunities to invite others into our world and share with them the joy we see before us. And we miss opportunities to be invited into their world as well. This little boy was sharing with me the pure joy he felt playing with these new baby pigs. The laughter from his heart helped me to understand his personality. This life brings him great joy and my joy was increased through his introduction into a world I could not have entered on my own.

Hospitality is inviting others into your world. Helping them to understand what brings you joy and allowing them to experience your joy. As a guest in someone else's world you can begin to respond to their personality differently as you watch their spirit being filled. Your spirit will be touched by what you see, hear, accept and appreciate from the experience. The spirit is amazing in its ability to respond to the spirit of another.

Extend your hospitality toward others as an invitation for them to enter your world and discover what makes your spirit whole. Your spirit will be moved as it shares joy with others. Hospitality deepens our understanding of others and makes the spirit smile!

Questions to ponder:
When have I experience unexpected hospitality?
How have I shown hospitality toward others?
What has my spirit learned from random acts of kindness?

What Does This Mean?

৵৵

I waited patiently for the Lord; he turned to me and heard my cry. He lifted me out of the slimy pit, out of the mud and mire; he set my feet on a rock and gave me a firm place to stand. He put a new song in my mouth, a hymn of praise to our God. Many will see and fear and put their trust in the Lord.
—*PSALM 40:1-3*

৵৵

(This reflection followed a disaster in our community, a flood in June of 2008)

I am writing today with a very heavy heart. The flood disaster has caused so much pain and sorrow over the last week and my heart cries out with many questions. These questions seem to be on the minds of others, as well. Perhaps the biggest question has been what does this mean? A question I have heard several times over the past few days. Can we sit with this question a few minutes as I write and you read?

Over the past week I have asked many people to tell me what is getting them through this, where they are getting their strength from, what it is that supports them in this difficult time? Their answers have overwhelmingly been, God. No long explanations, rather a short to the point answer, God. There has then been a pause in our conversation followed by an admission of questions and curiosities that run through their minds. We have common questions and curiosities, but share a strong connection in the belief that God still exists in the midst of all of this.

The next question we must struggle with is this, is that enough? Is it enough for us to trust that God knows the way he will take care of each of us in our times of struggle and we must be patient, we must wait, we must trust? Is it enough to trust that we are not alone, and simply take one day at a time, searching out the blessing in each day.

As I sat downtown the other day at lunchtime watching the people mill around the streets examining the flood waters I was surprised by what I saw. I expected to see sorrowful faces. I expected to hear angry voices. Instead I saw people smiling at one another, nodding their heads in understanding to one another. I heard people say they were doing what they had to do, one day at a time. I heard people asking, "How can I help", "what can I do", "who needs help". These questions were sincere in their desire to be of service to those in need.

I have watched people gather together to organize relief efforts. I am grateful for the organizations throughout this nation reaching out to disaster areas, but I am also grateful for the human spirit alive and well in our community, which has drawn the strength needed to reach out to one another here in this community. It appears as though the hearts of individuals being called to serve are overflowing with compassion and the hearts of those receiving this compassion seem to be overflowing with gratitude. Bonds are being built between people once strangers, now friends, family. Have we been given the opportunity to be reintroduced to our brothers and sisters in Christ?

I cannot begin to address the questions about why this happened, why one household and not the other, or the other questions that come with any tragedy, but I can at least take the time to listen to what God is offering me in this experience. A chance to share my faith with others, a chance to have my faith strengthened by others, a chance to see first-hand the way we are all connected in this world.

What does this mean? I am not sure anyone can answer this question with a universal answer. Each of us has to look to the events that happen in life for the personal meaning and the collective meaning. We must use the events of our life journey to exercise our spiritual health. Tried, stretched, and tested the spirit within has great power. The spirit will not be broken.

Even though the responses to the many questions have expressed a lack of understanding of the reason these events have happened in our lives, they seem to have consistent faith in God, trusting that God knows. In the midst of the devastation that has come to our community the human spirit perseveres. It is my prayer that our community will recover with a renewed sense of who our neighbors are and a stronger spirit of unity.

Questions to ponder:
What have my experiences been with community disasters/tragedies?
What strengthens my faith to persevere difficult times?

Have You Met My Spirit?

૭૭

*May the fruit of the spirit provide the introduction of
your spirit.*
*The fruit of the Spirit is love, (loving) joy, (joyful) peace,
(peaceful) patience, (patient) kindness, (kind) goodness,
(good) faithfulness, (faith-filled) gentleness, (gentle) and
self-control (self-controlled). Against such things there is
no law.* —GALATIANS 5: 22-23, *parenthesis added.*

૭૭

I hope this letter finds you welcoming the season of new life. It is always amazing to me the way spring gently opens before my eyes. God introduces spring with such subtlety. Southerly breezes melt away the cold covering from the earth and blades of grass push forth adding color to the dark soil. The smell of the air changes and we sense the presence of spring in our midst. Spiritual introductions can be subtle, too. I invite you to reflect with me on this topic.

I stayed with a friend and parish nurse colleague before attending a conference. She had recently moved into a new home and invited me to stay with her. This woman has such a gently spirit and I was delighted to consider the extra time that would allow me to spend with her. I had known her for over 7 years and I count her as a dear friend. We met up with another parish nurse colleague for dinner and had a lovely time together. Our conversation was rich with history. I heard stories about where they grew up, where they worked, where they got their education, their families, and much more. We laughed and enjoyed each other's company. So where is this story going? Let me continue, here is where the reflection part comes in.

We returned to her home and she gave me a tour of her home, pictures of her family adorned the walls. Her home was filled with signs of spring. Her Christian faith was expressed in verses and artwork displayed for her guests to enjoy. The room she offered me was warm and welcoming. She made sure I had everything I needed for a good night sleep. As I crawled into bed I began to review our conversations from dinner. I could not remember one thing she had told me. How could that be? I have known this woman for over 7 years. Some of the information she shared was new, but some I remembered as she began to share. Now here I am only hours later in her home unable to recite one thought! What was the matter with me?

Then it occurred to me. If I had to introduce her to a group of people I would stumble with some of the details of her journey, of her life, but I could easily introduce her spirit. What I would be able to confidently say in describing her is that she is kind, considerate, compassionate, grateful, faithful, unselfish, and passionate about caring for others. I have known her spirit for 7 years. Her spirit is what really matters.

I began to understand my inability to remember people's names. I am terrible at it. You may even know this about me. It is not because I do not care about your name; it is because I care about your spirit. I want to know your spirit. There is a song by the group Point of Grace entitled, "How You Live: Turn up the Music". I love the message in this song. Here are a few lines of the chorus, "…cause it's not who you knew, and it's not what you did, it's how you lived". The way you live is what people remember. Your spirit tells who you are. I encourage you to find an opportunity to listen to this song. It reminds us to release our spirit and live fully every single day.

Over the years I have used an exercise with groups of people asking them to write a personal introduction for me to use if I were introducing them to a group of strangers. They are asked to write down what they want others to know about them. I would be willing to bet that if I would have asked you to do this exercise before reading this reflection, you would respond the way most people do. They put on paper, where they live, where they work, what their educational background is, and/or what their role is in their family, community, or place of employment. Although, each of these activities contributes to the development or stifling of one's spirit, they have very little to do with who you are spiritually, and therefore who you really are.

The hospitality shared by my dear friend helped me to understand more clearly the importance of meeting the spirit of an individual. I will be a little kinder with myself for my inability to remember details about someone's life and a little more focused on the spirit within the individuals I meet along life's journey.

I believe God's message also encourages me to remember my own spirit yearning to be introduced and the characteristics and actions I want people to remember. I invite you to begin your introductions in the future by considering this question, have you met my spirit?

Questions to ponder:
What kind words best describe my spirit?
How easy is it to introduce my spirit to a
group of strangers?
What will others remember about me?

A Woven World

𝒮𝒮

Remember color is more vibrant when outlined in dark colors. Let not the darkness of this world dull your vibrancy rather let it enhance the color of your spirit.

𝒮𝒮

One day I sat quietly in a small restaurant having an early breakfast alone. The sun was just beginning to peak over the horizon as I walked into the restaurant. Yet as I sat at my table I observed a buzz of conversation. There was rich laughter and soft whispers in the room. The scene was rich with information about the human condition. Let me reflect for you on the topic of a woven world.

The young woman behind the counter of stools filled with early risers walked briskly back and forth with her pot of coffee or plate of food. She smiled and laughed. She asked them questions about their lives, the football stats, the weather and the headlines in the newspaper. Another waitress greeted customers with a welcoming smile. One couple came in and she welcomed them announcing they would have someone else serving them this particular morning rather than herself. She made them comfortable with light bantering.

I could not help but think about the imprint these women were making on these people's lives. They were setting the tone for the day. They were allowing their joy in their work to spill over onto their customers and the customers loved it. You could see relationships developing through these interactions. These women were sharing their spiritual gifts of conversation and listening and were very professional about their work.

For me there is no separation between professional and non-professional. There is rather professionalism, which can be exhibited in all work. The act of professionalism sets apart those who embrace their work as a gift from God from those who merely focus on a name, title, or letters behind their name. When someone shares their spirit through their work with others they are taking on full responsibility for the impact their work has on those around them. They are skilled and competent in what they do and perform their work with great passion.

Another experience of occurred on that same day, which clinched for me the need to share this message about the weaving of lives. A colleague at work brought an incredibly beautiful quilt she had created. It was intricate in detail, full of color and stories. From bird houses to vegetables in baskets, brick paths through flowers to hanging baskets, bird bathes to waddling ducks, and wheelbarrows to bridges everything was woven together in one perfect picture. Each scene was separate yet connected to the other.

We are like that. Each of us is separate and perfectly woven to be the person God has created and our work together with those around us creates the tapestry of life we live in. Designed by God and fulfilled by each of us embracing our own unique role in the bigger picture.

My spirit is nurtured by the work I do when I put my heart and soul into it. Your spirit can be nurtured by the work you do, too. So if you are hung up on the letters behind your name, the numbers of years of education you have, the amount of pay you receive or the prestige you receive from others, I encourage you to come down for you are at great risk of falling. If you believe your job is menial, worthless I encourage you to let go of any stigma that burdens your work and stand up so as not to be buried because regardless of the type of work you do if you do your job with competence, joy and spirit the work you do is an integral part of the woven world. Indeed, you add color to the tapestry of life.

Questions to ponder:
What do I bring to the tapestry of life?
How do I exhibit professionalism in my work?
What makes my colors shine?

Go Ahead, Say It

ℒℒ

For God so loved the world that he gave His only Son
that we might have eternal life with him, JOHN 3:16

ℒℒ

One morning as I prepared for my walk I was deterred by these four words, GO AHEAD, SAY IT, stirring in my head. I had been preparing for a trip to Africa and by the time you read this reflection I will have long recovered from jetlag. Have you ever prepared for a trip and then felt the need to give someone a call, write letters to loved ones, or even prepare a will? Often times it is in our plans to leave our physical home that we begin to ponder what we want to happen before we leave our earthly home. I want to take the time to share with you a reflection on the topic of saying the hard stuff.

Perhaps it becomes clearer to us when we are planning a trip or are facing a change in our health, but we ultimately never know how things are going to turn out. Will the trip be safe? Will we be healed of our illness? Will our loved one recover? Just because we are more aware of our own mortality during these times this awareness does not make the topic any easier to talk about. There can be; a fear of saying the wrong thing or a desire to protect the one we love from knowing the dangers, risks, or prognosis of the situation. Based on my own experience, working with patients and families, the thoughts are already there. In some ways I think this heightened awareness can be a gift to us. A time for sharing love, laughter, tears, or fears more openly with those around us. Talking about it, rather than just thinking about it, provides a freedom to release any fear and begin the process of openly expressing one's feelings.

So, GO AHEAD, SAY IT. Well it is not that easy for some reason. I am having trouble getting onto this page exactly what I think God wants me to say because I am afraid these words will make you sad, make you angry, make you feel guilty, even make you cry. Though, as I continue to care about people who are grieving I am made even more aware of the urgency for saying what you want to say to those you care about.

After my brother-in-law died, I vividly remembered the last time I talked with him. He walked by my office and we waved at each other, he said he was on his way to see someone and wondered if he was in the right area. I nodded and simply said, "Yes, you're headed the right way". Do you think I ever wish I would have walked with him and shared more time in conversation? Absolutely! Every time I think about it. He was gone before I ever had a chance to say another word to him.

We all do this when someone dies. We review the last words we said. We can never predict when our last words will be shared, nor should we live in fear that every word might be our last. So what should we do? We should; GO AHEAD, SAY IT. Don't hold back on those feelings that want to be expressed. Don't leave out those gestures of kindness toward others. Don't hesitate to write letters of love to family members and friends. Don't put off thanking someone for all they have done for you over the years. When your spirit is moving you to visit someone, visit them. When your spirit moves you to call someone and you think you are too busy or they are too busy, call them. Celebrate the time you have together. Seek forgiveness when you have wronged someone. Tell someone if they have hurt you so that you can resolve the hurt, quite often the other person is unaware of the hurt they have caused and appreciate you telling them so that the heavy feeling in the relationship can be lifted.

One of the things that keeps coming into my mind as I seem to be pondering this whole idea of not knowing when my life will end, which seems to be particularly on my mind in light of my trip, is this; don't be silly, nothing is going to happen, people travel all the time, just forget it, don't make people worry, God is in control. The question following these thoughts is this; what is the worst that can happen by expressing my feelings to those I care about? My family and friends will know I love them. People in my life will know I am grateful for their presence. Maybe someone will read this reflection and be prompted to share openly their feelings about death and dying, their fears about being alone, or their need for support. If these are the worst things that can happen to us, why hesitate, GO AHEAD, SAY IT!

Here goes, I am thankful for the blessings of my family and friends. I am grateful for all the people who have touched my life. I love my community and my work. I hope to continue to serve others in need. Thank you for allowing me to reflect with you on the messages God sends me to share with you. Now that wasn't so hard after all. I think it is a good start! Do not worry about when your life will end or when your loved ones life will end, but rather live each day as if it were the last one you had to share with others on this earth and please tell those around you how much they mean to you.

Questions to ponder:
What prevents me from sharing my true feelings?
How hard is it for me to talk with family and
friends about death?
What hope to I have in eternal life?

Touches of Life

৯৬

*What do we live for, if it is not to make life less difficult
for each other?* —GEORGE ELIOT

৯৬

Spring represents new life. It is a meaningful season of the year for me, one that causes me to pause and reflect on my life and how it has been shaped over the years by others, by touches of life.

Countless people have been a part of my becoming who I am. I have been shaped through their instruction. Smoothed by their friction. Polished by their love. I am the person I am because of the many people who have brushed life with me. Many of those people will never know the impact they have had on my life, nor in many cases do I have a firm recollection of their presence.

Sometimes we brush up against another's life in a way that leaves us with questions about the interaction. Those who are kind to us in the grocery store, who look bewildered as they walk along the sidewalk, those who call at just the right moment of need, all brush our life with color, which adds to the rainbow within each of us.

I had a wonderful interaction with a young man I sat next to on a plane. He was in his early 20's, I imagine. As I sat next to him, he was looking longingly at a picture of a young woman on his cell phone. I was drawn to inquire about the woman and he shared with me his story of being home with his family and spending time with his girlfriend. He shared how she had been ill while he was home and how he had taken care of her. He was on his way to Baltimore for deployment orders, then on to Iraq where he would be stationed for the next 18 months. I thanked him for his service and for sharing with me a piece of his life story.

This young man has come to my mind many times since that encounter. He was instrumental in deepening my appreciation for the unique story within every person I meet. Many times I have been on a plane, bus, train or in a crowded room without talking with the person next to me. Yet, in this opportunity I was stirred to speak and met with an openness to share. I promised this young man I would pray for him and his family. This young man, a total stranger is now one of the many people on my prayer list.

Perhaps there are no strangers. Just those people we have not yet met. Only days after having had this interaction I noticed a young woman walking and she had such anger on her face. Our eyes met, just for that split second when you catch someone else's glance. It struck me for whatever reason, and then I quickly forgot about it. Hours later as I drove through town again I met her gaze once more. What are the odds of that happening? Meeting the glance of a stranger twice in the same day, hours apart, in different areas of the community. Stranger or someone I have not yet met? At any rate, she too has been added to my list of people to pray for.

These two incidents occurred just prior to a class I was attending in La Crosse, Wisconsin. My professor helped me make a connection between these encounters and how they impact my life. As he welcomed us back to the class he spoke of the need to show appreciation to others in our life for what they contribute to who we become. Then he thanked each of us for the way we had touched his life over the past weeks. What a wonderful gesture, to honor those we meet, however briefly, for all they offer to our journey in life. Our life is forever new with growth because we are in constant connection with others.

May the changing seasons of life be a reminder to you of the new life available each day through your encounters, however small, for each is a touch of life.

Questions to ponder:
Have I ever been surprised by a conversation with someone
I did not know?
How did they impact my life?
Have I ever prayed for someone I did not know? Why?
Why, not?

Something is Missing

❧

*A hug is a great gift, one size fits all and it's
easy to exchange.*
—CARYL WALLER KRUEGER

❧

The gardens are blooming and filled with a multitude of fragrances. Walking from one fragrance to the next I am reminded of my childhood as the delicate scent of fresh blooms take me instantly back to a slower quieter time and of being carried by my parents at the end of a long day of playing with my siblings. Today as I enjoy the faces of young children I often find myself feeling that something is missing.

It came to me one evening. What's missing? It is the gentleness of human touch. Everywhere I go I see new parents with so many convenient baby items. Wonderful new car seats, added safety features on walkers, swings and bouncy seats. What bothers me about these new items is there seems to be much less physical contact between parent and baby. Babies are securely belted into their car seats and carried to the car where they are then buckled in. When they arrive at their destination the seatbelt is released and the whole car seat is removed without ever having to touch the baby. The car seat then becomes the carrier rather than the parent.

Now this may seem like a wonderfully convenient way to transport a baby, but I worry about the lack of physical contact. In a restaurant one night a waitress set up a device that supports the car seat/carrier. Sort of a pre-high chair stage I guess. The baby continued to sit there during dinner, rather than on the lap of a parent, grandparent or sibling. There is something so tender about holding a baby in your arms that I worry not only about the babies lack of physical contact but also that the parent, grandparent or sibling is missing out on some of the most powerful feelings they will ever experience.

Please don't misunderstand me, I am not faulting new parents for taking advantage of the convenient baby products, but I want to caution them about this limited physical touch. This is not just a baby/parent phenomenon; I see it all over in many areas of human interaction. We limit hand shaking so that we do not come in contact with germs. We limit hugs for fear of having our intentions misinterpreted.

Human beings need touch. They need gentle touch. Elderly people often say one of the things they miss the most after losing a spouse is touch. Hugs, holding hands and gentle caresses are gone. Individuals in nursing homes often go for long periods of time without family members hugging them or holding their hand. What is it about the power of the human touch that makes us long for it when it is absent in our lives? I believe it is the spiritual connection that occurs when we touch someone.

I believe it is hard to know how the lack of touch will impact our children in the future. It simply seems as though it will create a barrier of spirit to spirit connections with others as we often see when our elderly long for that touch to lift their spirit.

Consider the way Jesus interacted with children. Pictures of Jesus with children depict him holding them in his arms or placing his hand on their heads. Jesus' touch was healing to all who received it. I believe that the power of the spirit within each of us has the potential to heal those with whom it is fortunate to touch, regardless of age. As for convenience, babies are well worth every ounce of effort put forth for their care and if we focus on the miracle that they are it will not matter how convenient life is. I pray that the healing power of gentle touch will never be missing from your life at any age.

Questions to ponder:
What can I learn from a simple handshake?
What comfort can be offered by a gentle hug?

CHAPTER 7

Change

A Way to Live

Live life with a smile upon your face
For you are destined for a better place
Though I have gone to get things ready
Look to the sky, keep your eye steady
Upon the Father looking down with love
The one who waits for you above
With open arms full of grace
And a smile upon his face

Drop the Rock

ᴥ

*Commit you way to the Lord; trust in him and he will
do this: He will make your righteousness shine like the
dawn, the justice of your cause like the noonday sun.*
—PSALM 37:5-6

ᴥ

During the last week of May, I attended a retreat in Door County, Wisconsin. I was co-leading a retreat and took the opportunity to participate in the various activities as well. The first night, we were asked to write upon a stone that which was holding us down, burdening us, or preventing us from experiencing peace, joy, God's love. We were instructed to then carry our rock with us to Peninsula State Park the next morning and drop the rock into the bay. Sometimes an activity as simple as dropping a rock into the water can have a deeper message. Let this be my topic for reflection.

The story begins with an explanation of how a woman's mother, as a teenager, wanted to see how deep the water was in a rock quarry. She decided to jump into the water holding onto a rock. As she did she found herself sinking deeper and deeper into the dark water. She panicked at first not knowing what to do. Then she realized that she need only to release the rock and she would be saved. The leader went on to describe the way many of us continue to hang onto things that cause us pain and suffering. We carry things that burden us needlessly. So she invited us to ponder on that which was dragging us deeper into the depths of darkness. What weight did we carry that needed to be dropped so that our spirit would not die from its weight? That was the question we were to reflect on before morning.

The next morning I wrote a word on my rock. Self-doubt. There it was, the weight I wanted to unload, to drop into the water asking God to release me from the heaviness it represented in my heart. We began to hike along the shores of Peninsula State Park and during a quiet reflective time we were directed to drop the rock into the water. I sat quietly, waiting (for the right moment I guess). I actually smiled to myself thinking how will I know it is the right time? I wondered, 'isn't right now the right time?' 'Why wasn't it something I did right away, even before I paused to sit down?'

So I reached into my pocket and gave it a fling and wouldn't you know it, it didn't make the water! It went click and landed among the thousands of rocks on the shore. One of the other women in the group heard it and looked my way and we laughed under our breath (it was after all suppose to be a time of silent reflection).

How symbolic! Sometimes you can try to get rid of things, drop them from your mind, remove them from your heart, but they really do not get completely dropped. Now I had a rock somewhere amongst the rocks on the shoreline with a burden I had hoped to drop. I began to search for my burden. White stones of all shapes and sizes formed the shoreline and I wondered how I would ever find it. I thought to myself, 'maybe it is dropped far enough to be effective. Perhaps God has forgiven me for carrying this burden and has allowed me to be rid of it'.

Just then it showed up. There it was again for me to pick up. I was faced with a choice. I could put it back in my pocket for another place and time or I could give it another fling to represent a desire to be rid of the weight it imposed on my heart. I chose to give it a fling realizing that even when we drop the rocks that weigh us down they might surface again and we will have to choose whether we will continue to carry the rock or drop it into deeper water.

Suddenly, the refrain of a song came to mind. The song was, *Come to Me, All Who Are Weary,* by Dan Schutte, and it is based on chapter 11 of Matthew's gospel. The words of the refrain are, "come unto me all who are weary and find rest for your soul, come to me all who are burdened you shall learn from me". Indeed I was learning even through the process of dropping my rock.

The ritual of dropping a rock with a burden attached to it signifies a desire to prepare ones heart for transformation. One at a time, each of us can drop the rock(s) that weigh us down and prepare our heart for God's transformation to take place deep within finding the peace and joy of living in his love. Go ahead, drop the rock.

Questions to ponder:
What burdens to I carry?
How many times have I picked them up again?
How can I dump them for good into the loving arms of God?

Breaking the Cycle

୨୧

Have I not commanded you? Be strong and courageous.
Do not be terrified; do not be discouraged, for the Lord
your God will be with you wherever you go. —JOSHUA 1:9

୨୧

The mountains were beautiful once again. The weather had been in the 30's. The snow on the slopes, though minimal, was well groomed and conditions were favorable for some excellent skiing. It was the setting for a perfect Colorado vacation, however, I found myself in the midst of a very poor sleep cycle. I want to reflect with you about the difficulties of breaking the cycle.

Our sleep is so important to our overall health. Each of us has our own requirement for adequate sleep, but research has shown that on average most people need 7-8 hours of sleep to renew their strength and repair tissue at the cellular level. Well, this was not happening for me in the mountains.

After the first night of waking every hour through the night I shrugged it off and blamed it on the altitude. After the second night I surmised it was all the excitement of being in the mountains. The third night I decided it must be the strange noises so I pulled out the earplugs. The fourth night I announced that it must be because I was eating more vegetables and less dessert! Waking after night number five there wasn't the least bit of humor in my speculation about why I was not sleeping. I was in a very foul mood. What was going on? Why couldn't I sleep? I wanted to sleep! I needed to sleep! I felt terrible, physically, emotionally, and spiritually. I became frustrated to think that my vacation time was being interrupted by a very poor sleep cycle.

As nightfall approached I began expecting to have a bad night. Fear of not sleeping filled my mind, consumed my thoughts and affected my ability to function. I was downright crabby about the fact that I was not sleeping and determined there was nothing I was going to do about it. I was helpless to make a change. *I was helpless to make a change.* That is when it hit me. God was using this experience for me to consider how hard it is to break a negative cycle. There is an overwhelming sense of helplessness when you enter a negative cycle. You feel trapped. To make an effort to break the cycle seems hopeless. He was using this experience for me to communicate this message to you.

How often do we get into a negative cycle, whether it be sleeping, eating, lack of exercise, failure to communicate appropriately with family, friends or co-workers, reduced enthusiasm about our work, or any other action or attitude that impacts our life? And, more importantly how do we get out of a negative cycle? I will venture to say in regard to the first question that sometimes slipping into a bad cycle comes subtly over time. You may not even notice the cycle developing. You might let down your guard against negative thoughts, decide to skip a day of exercise or forgo a healthy food choice and somehow slip into a second or third time not realizing a negative cycle has begun.

When you enter a negative cycle there is a sense of helplessness. You feel trapped. You feel hopeless. Any effort to break the cycle seems overwhelming.

In my nights of sleeplessness, the words from Matthew 11:28, "come to me all of you who are weary and carry heavy burdens, and I will give you rest", came to mind. This was the answer I found in my heart, the way I was going to break the cycle. I turned my weariness over to God. Prayer, reading his word, and reflecting in the silence provided me with rest.

When you find yourself in a negative cycle, trust that God's strength is what you need to overcome. He is not going to leave you alone to figure it out on your own. He will guide you and protect you as you work your way back into a positive cycle, one that builds you up and improves your health, body, mind and spirit. Listen to your experience, God might be trying to send you a message even in your sleeplessness.

Questions to ponder:
Am I in a negative cycle right now?
What do I do when I get into a negative cycle?
How will God help me overcome and break into a positive cycle?

Called to Grow

ℒℒ

A ship in harbor is safe, but that is not what ships are built for. —WILLIAM SHEDD

ℒℒ

I wonder if the flowers of spring have as much resistance to growing as I do sometimes. Have you ever dreamed about something and then been encouraged to do something about it? Twice now in the past few weeks I have been encouraged to step out in faith and pursue one of my dreams. I want to share my reflection with you about being called to grow with the hope that it will inspire you to grow.

In celebration of my 50th birthday, my brother asked me what I wanted to do in the next 5 years. I shared a couple of goals I had for the future. Two weeks later I made a contact with a woman who shared a resource with me for beginning the process for attaining one of my goals. Okay, so I stated a goal out loud in the presence of family and then I had a woman whom I had never met before share a resource with me that could get the ball rolling. Does it need to be clearer than that? I am being called to grow in my faith that God is leading me to reach a goal that he has set for my life journey.

Ready, set, grow…into my mind comes fear, doubt, time constraints, work demands, excuses. I can't do it. I don't want to do it. It will be hard work. At the same time these negative thoughts and excuses are rolling around in my head so too is a song by Matthew West entitled, *The Motions*. In the refrain are the following words, "I don't want to spend my whole life asking; what if I had given everything, instead of going through the motions". These words were doing battle with my negative thoughts and excuses.

What's repeating in your head? What are you being called to do? God tells us he will grow us into the purpose he has called us for. I believe He will not take us where he will not sustain us. What is there to fear in growing? Why the reluctance? More importantly for me, what if my time runs out before I complete my purpose on earth, the task I am being called to?

Isn't it easier to avoid times of growth? Maybe. Yet with every struggle that I have ever had in moving toward that which I had been called something good, something rich has been experienced. The struggles have added a deep richness to my life that I would have never missed, I suppose, had I not followed through, but today I cannot imagine my life without the achievement of each goal. I have been privileged to have others share their stories of struggle with me. They share the ways in which they overcame their fears, faced the challenges. They share with me the impact the struggle has had on their faith, on the depth of their spiritual understanding of the bigger picture.

I wonder if the tulips doubt whether they will be able to push through the packed soil, provide enough color to cause us to smile with awe. So when thoughts like, I'm not good enough, I'm not smart enough, rich enough, talented enough, not _____ enough (you fill in the blank)come to your mind let them be all the more reason to step out and grow.

Having made the decision I needed to consider, well then where do I start? It is up to me to make the next move. God has presented the opportunities for goal setting, inspiring people surround me with confidence, and potential resources have been identified. God is preparing me to grow, to look toward the future and ask, where do I start. Not as a doubtful question but as a guide for outlining a process. Today I pray for direction to accomplish the work God has started in me and to begin to let go of the doubts and fears so that I will not have to wonder, "what if I had given everything, instead of going through the motions".

Questions to ponder:
What would happen if spring resisted the struggle
for new growth?
What if the flowers of spring chose not to push through the
cold, packed soil to add beauty and define
God's presence in our lives?
Am I giving everything or am I going through the motions?

The Watchful Eye of God

*And surely I am with you always, to the very
end of the age. —MATTHEW 28:20*

Could there be anything more inspiring than being on the top of
a mountain at 20 degrees below zero (actual temperature, burr)
with skis on your feet and witnessing the *Watchful Eye of God*? If
there is I cannot imagine it. Let me share with you the message I
received on this particular frigid morning.

The weather had been representative of the great burdens
we bare in life. There had been heavy snowfalls, gusting winds
and extremely cold temperatures in our first week of being in
the mountains of Colorado. These weather extremes could also
be used to describe the feelings in our hearts when we are experiencing stress, grief or fear, when we bare heavy burdens.

I could not help but notice that the majestic pines seemed
to extend their branches willingly taking on the burden of the
heavy snowfall and demonstrating to me the strength they have
gained through experience. The smaller trees drooped slightly
lower than the mature trees and seemingly taking their cues
from the mature trees to hang in there and support the load
where courageous in their efforts. The branches held their burden upward as if they were offering it up. Even when the bows
drooped in the middle the ends were slightly curved upward
waiting for the Watchful Eye of God to shine warmth upon their
burden, trusting that the heaviness would soon be melted away.
Then with the release of their burden the branches would be
able to spring back to life extending upward even more in praise
of God's faithfulness.

Nature displayed the feelings of my heart. Grief, fear and stress were some of the emotions being experienced during this trip. You see, we had lost a dear friend and for many of you reading this letter I imagine you can relate to the kind of heaviness I am describing. On this particular morning though it seemed as though God wanted to remind me through nature of his constant, loving, watchful eye and that he would not allow my soul to break under the burden. I believe God wanted me to know that he would always be there to provide support and encourage my strength in managing the heaviness of my heart.

So, what about this watchful eye *witnessing*? What am I talking about anyway? Well it was amazing. I will try with all my heart to use words to describe what I saw, what we saw, not once but twice! A few days before this particularly frigid morning we were skiing and the sky was totally gray, sort of a solid soft gray (no billowy clouds). As we arrived at the top of the mountain the sun was trying to burn through the gray. Soon there was an easy outline of the sun behind the veil of grayness. It was striking. As we looked closer we could see a complete thin ring of light. This ring of light shown away from the center and it looked like an eye complete with a pupil, an iris and the white sclera. Never before had either of us seen anything like it. I remarked to my husband that God was watching over us. It would have been impossible to capture on film so we allowed it to be imprinted on our mind. Amazing! (Words do not describe it).

Now only days later we were standing on top of this frigid mountain and we looked to the sky to witness another *sky sign*. This time the sky was crystal blue. The sun burned brightly and at 3, 6, 9 and 12, as if on a clock, there were stripes of rainbow. They were curved reaching toward connection, making a perfect circle in the sky. Once again looking just like an eye!

The message God honed in on with amazing clarity, the message I was grateful to receive, was this, whether our world is dark and gray or bright blue and filled with sunshine we must remember that God sees our burden. God cares about our heaviness. God strengthens us and at the right time melts away our pain, our suffering, our burden. It is then that we will graciously allow our lightened arms to be lifted like the branches of the trees in praise toward the *Watchful Eye of God*.

Questions to ponder:
How do I know that God is watching over me?
What signs do I witness through nature
that God is present?
Am I currently weighed down with a burden I would like
God to melt away?

Under Pressure

⁘

May the God of hope fill you with all joy and peace as
you trust in him, so that you may overflow with hope by
the power of the Holy Spirit. —ROMANS 15:13

⁘

As I sit down to write this reflection for your reading, I maintain that God selects the topic. I am writing you today somewhat "under pressure" and it occurred me as I pondered topics that God wants me to share my experience and feelings about being under pressure in synchronization with the season. The fall whispers a message of slowing down, bringing the hustle and bustle of the summer to an end, while preparing for the chill of winter. The season is a reminder to us that those home improvements, visits to friends and good intentions need to be completed soon or they will either have to wait until next spring or be forgotten forever. So the benefits of slowing your life down with the slowing of the season can potentially make you feel under pressure to achieve the goals you had set earlier in the year.

Have you ever told someone that you "work better under pressure"? Being under pressure can be a positive force for some activities. I would have to admit that I have used this "work better under pressure" statement a time or two. I tend to become more organized and efficient when the clock is ticking. A certain amount of stress can be motivating and even protective in saving us from physically harmful situations. I would also have to admit there have been times when the pressure reached a level too high to be efficient. It is in times like this when I am forced to pause for personal reflection about where the motivation to complete my projects or tasks is being drawn from. The stress level reaches a potentially harmful level.

There is a point where too much stress causes feelings of insecurity, inadequacy, and inferiority, and when these feelings fill my mind I become unable to accomplish my job with any level of efficiency. Do you know this feeling? It can stop you in your tracks. You may feel paralyzed, unable to focus your attention long enough to finish your task, which leaves you feeling more overwhelmed. Have you ever felt overwhelmed by the number of commitments you have in your life? In my estimation it is this feeling of being overwhelmed that is a red flag to stop and reflect on the health of my spirit and just where my motivation is coming from.

Is God leading my life or have I created my own agenda? Here is the question I had to ask myself in the last few weeks. Feeling overwhelmed and seemingly unable to accomplish my agenda, I suffered feelings of insecurity and inadequacy. Red flag for personal reflection fully flying I needed to take a good look at where my motivation was coming from. I realized that I had become somewhat insensitive to the daily prompting of God and was rather rushing into the day and my work with my own agenda. Keeping to my schedule and checking my lists had become extremely important to me. I suddenly felt as though I had so much on the list that I was seriously neglecting the work God was calling me to do.

Personal reflection is difficult. It can be facilitated by sharing your feelings with a trusted friend, a friend who can listen and allow you to hear what you have whirling around in your mind. A trusted friend can offer you an objective view when you are looking for one. This trusted friend is not a person who flaunts advice without permission, but rather allows you the time you need to identify for yourself what will work best for you in solving the questions in your mind. I needed to return my trust back to being lead daily by God without concern about my own agenda. I clearly know through my own experiences that God lovingly prompts us and places us where we need to be at the precise moment necessary when we fully turn our lives over to him.

It is our over stretched schedules and busy minds that cloud our ability to see what our spirit is prompting us to do with our lives. Having discovered this dilemma I needed to consider how I had gotten off track and more importantly how I could get back on track. I realized I had developed a fear of saying "no". Yet, when I say "yes" there is always an opposing "no" being offered. Here is what I mean. When you say "yes" to committees, individuals, or extra hours you are also saying "no" to time for spiritual rest and renewal, and potentially "no" to God's prompting.

Please understand that I am not suggesting that I will or that you should say "no" to all requests from individuals or community needs, but rather that you evaluate how often you are saying "yes" to your spiritual health. Balance is so important in life. When God is motivating you to help others you will have the energy you need to accomplish the job. However, I would venture to say that if you are exercising your own agenda without God moving your life you will be sapped of energy, unable to accomplish the job, and ultimately damaging your spirit.

If you find yourself "under pressure" check in with the feelings you might be experiencing. Remember that feelings of being overwhelmed are a red flag for considering the health of your spirit and the motivating force behind the pressure. One of God's many promises to each of us is that God will not call you to action without giving you the strength you need to accomplish it. Thank you, Lord, for renewing my spirit through the writing of this reflection.

Questions to ponder:
How do I know when I am under pressure?
How will I say "yes" to my spiritual needs?

Daily Renewal

୬୬

Forgiveness is one way to burn through the emotions that
cloud the goodness of the heart.

୬୬

Oh the joy of springtime. Crisp days of early spring will slowly give way to warmer days. Springtime is a time of renewal. The earth comes forth with newness of life. I want to write to you about the opportunity we receive every day, all year long for renewal, daily renewal.

This morning as I stepped out onto the front porch to start my day with a brisk walk I was mesmerized by the sunrise. I glanced at it initially and was beckoned to stop and watched in awe as light gently reached into the clear blue sky. The tiny rays were slowly casting light onto the horizon, spilling color into the darkness of night and calling forth a new day. The light quietly snuck out from behind the earth as if afraid of waking the world from its peaceful state. The sun rose with a message of tender renewal. A new day awaits its opportunity and once again the brilliance of light pours over the earth renewing the world with freshness. What once was dark becomes bright.

There was noticeable warmth on my face as the sun rose and it reached into my heart, warming my heart as if understanding my need for personal renewal. It reminded me of the daily renewal offered to each of us by God. The sunrise was an invitation to renew my heart that morning. Every day we are given the opportunity to begin the day with a fresh start, a clean slate, without fear, leaving behind the events of yesterday. Every day we can ask God to walk with us, lead us, and tend our needs.

This message may come easily to us when the sun rises into a clear sky, but what about the cloudy or fogging mornings. How does the sunrise on a cloudy or foggy day speak to us? What might it be encouraging us to consider about our heart, about our life? After the sun had fully risen and the glow in the sky was so intense that I could not look at it I wondered about this question. This is the answer I received. When there are clouds or fog present at sunrise we still know that there is a bright sun beyond the clouds or fog working to burn through and bring us light. Some light does make it through, but it is limited by the presence of the clouds or fog. Our hearts are inherently good but sometimes the goodness is not allowed to come forward because there is resentment, anger, bitterness, guilt or shame blocking the goodness of our heart from being shared with those around us.

Even though these emotions may block the goodness of our heart we have the promise of God that he will answer our cry for help. We can call out; "Create in me a clean heart, O God, and renew a right spirit within me" Psalm 51:10. We can be assured that he will bring forth the goodness and allow the resentment; anger, bitterness, shame and guilt to be burned off like the clouds and fog.

Prompted by the sunrise, something else came to mind for me this particular morning. As I walked I thought about the differences in the sunrise and sunset. I have visualized the sunrise and sunset many times with a strong appreciation for their beauty. I must admit I have marveled at more sunsets than sunrises, as I am not the best morning person. There are similar qualities in the coloring and ability to capture your attention with intense awe, but one of the differences I pondered was the time it takes each to occur. Let me explain. Often people will pour out onto the beach to watch the sunset. They arrive and get their cameras ready and within a split second the last rays of light flash across the water and the Kodak moment is gone. Gone in an instant. Much like the day. The residual light lingers for a long time casting streaks of color across the sky with shouts of vibrancy. The lingering helps us to slow down for the day.

The actual sunrise seems to be slower than the sunset. The sun's rays peak forth and nudge the world into wakefulness. The sun creeps onto the horizon almost as if being slowly pulled into the sky. The color in the sky is pure, soft, and new. We can choose to begin our days slowly like the sunrise by giving our day to God each morning welcoming the opportunity for daily renewal, rather than forcing ourselves upon the day. We can allow God to bring us to the place we need to be instead of forging forward based on our own desires for the day.

I invite you to seek out God's promise of creating within you a new heart one free from resentment, anger, bitterness, guilt or shame. You can do this one-day at a time. Taking that opportunity for daily renewal and celebrating each new day with a fresh new start. As we read in Psalm 118:24, "This is the day the Lord has made. Let us rejoice and be glad in it." This psalm does not say yesterday, three weeks from now, last month or tomorrow, but rather today, everyday is the day that the Lord has given us and we are to rejoice and be glad to be a part of it with a renewed hope in uncovering the goodness in our heart.

Questions to ponder:
When was the last time I reflected on the
meaning of the sunrise?
What clouds my heart?
How can God renew my heart and my life?

What's Next?

ℒℒ

*Even youths will become exhausted, and young men will
give up. But those who wait on the Lord will find new
strength. They will fly high on wings like eagles. They will
run and not grow weary. They will walk and not faint.*
—ISAIAH 40:30-31

ℒℒ

Nature and the changing season provide signals of what we can
expect to happen next. From the darkening sky, which indicates
a rainstorm, to the turning colors of the leaves reminding us of
the coming winter months, these signs help us prepare for what's
next. I want to reflect with you about some things we cannot
prepare for and the ways we might determine what's next.

As we go through life we set goals based on our dreams and
desires. We pray for guidance in knowing which job to pursue, which career to follow. We consider the characteristics we
desire in a mate and make plans for our future relationships
and the creation of a family. We dream about places we want to
live, things we want to see. We set out to reach these goals and
dreams with great determination and hope.

Sometimes, however, our best-laid plans do not develop the
way you want them to. Maybe you were not accepted into the
school you had been looking forward to attending. Perhaps you
do not find the mate of your dreams. It could be your funds do
not allow you to set out and see the places you long to see. The
pregnancy you long for is not happening or maybe the love of
your life, your soul mate has died and is no longer with you to
fulfill the plans you had made with them for the future.

What's next? How do you go forward when all you have dreamed of or set out to do has been interrupted, totally blocked or is simply not developing? How do you begin to make sense of the unanswered prayers? When your spirit is defeated, filled with confusion and sorrow, how do you discover what's next?

Have you ever found yourself asking this question? I think it is easier to ask, why, Lord, why me, Lord, or even why not, Lord? We know unfortunately all too well from life experiences that we never really get the answer we want to these questions. I wonder if, when the time is right, the better question to ask is indeed what's next, Lord? How do you begin to let go of the hopes and dreams you had for the future and allow yourself to create new goals, hopes and dreams based solely on the plans God has for your future?

I believe that before you can ask this question and pursue the answer you must first allow yourself to grieve. Grieve your disappointment, loss, and sorrow. Tell your story. Tell your story to a good listener not someone who will try to fix you or take away your pain, but someone who will walk with you through this time of difficultly allowing you to experience all that you need to experience. You must allow yourself to feel what you feel. As I work with individuals who are experiencing loss or disappointments they tell me it helps to talk about it. Sometimes weeks and months later, they still need to tell their story as part of the process for going forward.

Once you begin to process your response to those inter-rupted goals and dreams you can begin to ask the question, what's next and open yourself up to what life presents to you. The process is not easy by any means. Opening yourself up to express your feelings is challenging enough, but to let go of the hopes and dreams you had set for the future can be very painful. We live in a society that does not honor pain as being helpful, a tool for growth, or having any positive effects. Our society does not like it when we express anger, when we cry in public, or when we shut ourselves down to the rat race of life for a time.

As you face the losses, interrupted dreams of your life your spirit cries out to be held, heard and mended. Finding someone to walk with you through your pain, someone you feel safe being with allows you to express each of your feelings openly without judgment. As the spirit is supported it will mend, slowly, with newness and strength unavailable to you without this experience.

Then comes the waiting, trusting, moments when you ask God, what's next? Remembering that you are not alone in any of your struggles is important as you look toward the future with hope for new goals and dreams just waiting to be followed. Listen to the silence, feel the breeze upon your face, wait upon the Lord. Your spirit will know what's next.

Questions to ponder:
Who do I trust to share my stories of loss or grief?
How can I ask and wait patiently for what's next?

Waves of Change

❧

We can rejoice, too, when we run into problems and tri-als, for we know that they are good for us—they help us learn to endure. And endurance develops strength of character in us, and character strengthens our confident expectation of salvation. And this expectation will not disappoint us. For we know how dearly God loves us, because he has given us the Holy Spirit to fill our hearts with his love. —ROMANS 5:3-5

❧

Sometimes we have great clarity of purpose and direction in our life. Then waves of change wash over us and we are suddenly in a fog. It was obvious to me while in Oregon with a hiking group one summer that God wanted me to visit this topic of dealing with the waves of change, a frequent topic of reflection, but one deserving of yet another look.

Have you ever been to Oregon? It was my first trip and the first thing I learned about Oregon is that you pronounce it Or-again, not Or-e-gon. The locals are quick to clarify the pronunciation. Clarity, here is a word that takes on a whole new meaning when you look over the edge of the boat into the water of Crater Lake. The depth of clarity is astounding. I was able to clearly see rocks that were 40-50 feet below the surface. We were told that researchers are able to view a black and white disk at 143 feet with the naked eye. Isn't it great when we can see our purpose in life with that depth of clarity? How often are you able to see your purpose clearly? Me? Not very!

Next we traveled to the coast where a dense fog rolled in over the beach. Perhaps this is an area of greater understanding for us. The fog in our life. The questions about what is my purpose in life, where am I going and what am I suppose to do with this (whatever it is going on in life right now) seem to be a little more familiar to me.

In the fog, the midst of not knowing, we often cling to what we do know; like the barnacles and mussels clinging to the lava rock in the tide pools along coastline. They seemed to be hanging on for dear life as the tide rolled in and out, as the waves of change washed over them beckoning them let go. I believe we hang on to the familiar when the waves of change threaten to roll over us again and again. We resist letting go. As I looked more closely at this phenomenon I noticed there were other creatures in the tide pools offering encouragement. They seemed to embrace the adventure, they seemed to have let go of the familiar. Indeed, they were flitting around gleefully, seemingly packing in all the sights of their temporary surroundings (as we did during this week of exploration and reflection, seeking renewal for our weariness).

While I sat in quiet reflection, 2 of my sisters giggled as they wondered if they would cause interference with my connection. In reality they always strengthen my connectedness. They remind me of that which remains constant during waves of change in life. What remains constant? Our creator giving us what we need at just the time we need it. God places people in our path that will support us during those foggy days; those who will walk with you on the foggy beach watching out for your safety, those who will listen to the turmoil in your heart without judgment, those who will offer you expertise to strengthen your relationships, those who will connect the dots between what we see in our lives and what we need in our lives. God will also bring us to places of awe and wonder reminding us of his power to overcome adversity replacing destruction with beauty-Crater Lake, allowing the surge of a waterfall to pool in quiet stillness, transforming the blowing grains of sand into waves of beauty across the landscape.

Yes, the waves of change will continue to be part of our lives. So, appreciate those times of clarity in your life when everything makes sense and you are confident in your direction and embrace those times when the fog moves in trusting God will provide you with what your spirit needs to be strong enough to ride the waves of change, forever touched by the adventure.

Questions to ponder:
What waves of change have I experienced?
How did God help me transform for the change?

CHAPTER 8

On the Road

Winter Lesson

It is not always that, which is in front of you that teaches you,
Sometimes it is that which is beside you.

Heading out into the cold air just before sunrise
Racing to the top of the hill to turn in time to visualize

Sneaking next to me rays of sunlight reflecting on the snow
The sunrise from a new perspective

Unfolding beside me instead of in front of me
Causing me to stop in my tracks and turn with appreciation

For all the beauty that is the sunrise

Lessons from a Scrabble Board

୨୨

Rich and poor have this in common: The Lord is the Maker of them all. —PROVERBS 22:2

୨୨

My husband and I had an opportunity to spend time together in Bayfield, WI, which is beautiful by the way and if you ever get the chance to visit there, please do. God's creation continues to unfold through the beauty found in nature. We enjoy playing scrabble so we often take this game with us when we travel. Each afternoon after hiking we pulled out the scrabble board. I want to reflect with you this month on some lessons from a scrabble board.

As the games began, I won, he won, I won, and he won. This all seemed fair. Then he won, he won, he won, he won, and he won. I am not kidding. Six in a row. This was not fair. Not only did he beat me, but he won by landslides of 65, 78, and over 100 points. This was not fair at all. He continued to get all the high point letters and I got the 1 point letters. He continued to be able to use all the point squares and I could only manage to fill in the pointless blank squares. Well let me tell you I was struggling to keep a positive attitude about playing a friendly game of scrabble. Before I knew it my focus was on winning the game, beating my husband, demonstrating my ability to win! I became more frustrated and he became sad and apologetic about playing perfectly good words.

I actually went to bed one night wondering whether or not there was a message being sent to me through the simplicity of a scrabble game. And indeed the message came to me slowly like a good word being played in just the right spot as to afford great insight (points).

I began to compare all that he had to work with to the little I had to work with. How often do we do this in life, look at what others have and compare it to what we have? I developed a really bad attitude toward the game. How often do we consider excuses for why we are copping a bad attitude? I forgot that I liked this game. How often do we lose sight of the reason we chose to enter into an activity, a relationship, a career? When things are going along smoothly it is easy for us to enjoy life. A little give and take here and there seems fair. Sometimes, however, life does not go along smoothly. Others seem to get all the breaks (scoring extra points). Others seem to have all the talents (the high counting letters).

It becomes very hard to maintain a positive attitude when life (or scrabble) becomes all about competition. When my husband offered to help me I became defensive and sported the 'I can do it myself' attitude. What was that all about? Don't we sometimes respond that way in life, as well, shrugging off offers of assistance for our pride? Truly, I was ashamed of myself for the way I was acting. I realized that he may not want to play with me if I continued with this attitude. I wanted in the worst way to have it not matter whether I was winning or losing. Negativity had a hold on me. I told myself to start finding the positive in every play. Isn't it the same with life? Shouldn't we try to find the positive in everything? Surely, I know I have encouraged others in the past to look for the positive points in difficult situations.

I am excited to have him read this reflection and realize that all of his suffering for my struggles was not in vain. I did learn something from those scrabble games that would not have been evident if we would have continued to win every other game. Without his participation in the game I would not have even played. There it was right in front of me playing out slowly and painfully. Life needs to be lived just as the game needs to be played with a certainty that there will be ups and downs, shining moments and ordinary moments. Can you imagine what life would be like if we did not have some shining moments to accent the ordinary moments? Can you imagine what life would be like if you only experienced shining moments? Certainly they would lose their meaning. The ordinary day to day activities should not be viewed as unimportant like a low counting letter. They are indeed what support the greater picture, the high points of life.

In God's eyes we are all given equal value and at different times in our lives we will experience smooth sailing and rough seas. Helping each other to make the most out of the circumstances (letters) we have been given will make all the difference in the world.

Games are made to be played, winning and losing. Life is meant to be lived, better or worse. When we get too caught up in competing with others for what we think is 1st place we miss the true meaning of the words, *playing* the game...*living* life. There is always something to be learned or gained even from a simple scrabble board.

Questions to ponder:
When have I copped a bad attitude because things were not going my way?
What value do the ordinary days have for my life?

The Tie that Binds

It is unfortunately only too clear that if the individual is not truly regenerated in spirit, society cannot be either, for society is the sum total of individuals in need of redemption. —C. G. JUNG

The Montana sky is as beautiful as you read about, but for me there was more to marvel at in Montana than the sky this past summer. I spent 7 days hiking with a group of 12 women. One of my sister's was on the trip and I had met three of the women from Illinois before, but the rest of the women I was meeting for the first time, as was the case with many of the women on this trip. It was a powerful week, filled with adventure. Upon my return, I wondered how by spending one week together we had created such strong feelings toward one another. Let me reflect on this question with you and explain what I have come to identify as the tie that binds.

When we come together to share a common interest there is automatically something to talk about and talk we did. This group of women had been looking forward to spending time together hiking through Glacier National Park for months. The things we had in common to begin with were a love of nature, a willingness to hike the terrain, and a desire to meet new people. What I found in my short time with these women, however, was that we had much more in common. There was a connection between us just waiting to be revealed.

Fast friendships were made, really fast friendships, a sisterhood you might say. Within 24 hours the group encountered an unexpected circumstance and I watched the entire group rise to the occasion, each being supportive in their words, actions and quiet presence. They were vigilant in supporting one another as if they were holding on to the rope that was a lifeline for the other. Have you ever experienced this kind of connection, when people around you, strangers even, gather to offer their presence, their unfailing strength to assure that you will be protected? Was this that *tie* that binds?

The idea of a rope connecting us together continued to reveal itself throughout the week. Even when it seemed we were sinking (literally, we had stepped out onto an iceberg on Iceberg Lake, actually onto one and then another for a photo and the first one started to sink as we attempted to return to the shoreline) one hand and then another reached out with assurance that they were not going to leave until everyone was safe.

Beyond the connection within our group was the tie that bound us to others. As I looked into the eyes of a woman, who was not part of our group, in crisis the connection was visible. We were connected spiritually. As I looked into her eyes I knew there was no way I could leave this woman on the side of the mountain in distress and in the eyes of the other women in my group I could see that neither could they. We acted as one to support her, each of us fulfilling a different role toward a common goal, to get her safely off the mountain.

As you can imagine there was so much to reflect on in Glacier National Park and believe me I did a lot of reflecting. The beauty of the park was astounding, beyond words. The flowers were in full bloom and the master gardener had created a canvas of amazing color for all us to admire and appreciate in our own way. The mountains were immense and I am convinced that mountain miles are longer than road miles (maybe they are marked as the crow flies)! The lakes offered a perfect mirrored reflection of the shorelines, the mountains, and of anyone looking in. I could have picked 25 topics for reflection, no doubt, but the message I am being called to share with each of you is this, there is a tie that binds us all together in this world.

We are not separate. We are one. We have a common thread that runs through each of us and although we may not see it at times, when we falter and need someone to hold a little tighter to the rope someone does. A sister, a friend, an acquaintance, a perfect stranger will get a tug on the rope that says to them, "hold on someone is falling". The tie binds. When we can identify the tie that binds us together, we can experience life with all of its joys and sorrows knowing we are not alone. We can live, love and laugh as we (the "chicks with sticks" hiking group) did on our trip to Montana. We are a lifeline for each other and the spirit within is the tie that binds.

Questions to ponder:
Have I ever felt the tug on my heart to reach out for someone struggling?
Has a stranger ever helped me in a surprising way?
How can I become more aware of the tie that binds us together?

Look Back

ೇೇ

Thou hast given so much to me, Give one thing more—
a grateful heart; Not thankful when it pleaseth me, As
if thy blessings had spare days; But such a heart, whose
pulse may be Thy praise. —GEORGE HERBERT

ೇೇ

I had the opportunity to participate in a Women's Hiking Retreat to Maine. We hiked for several days and saw beautiful views of God's creation. Much of the hiking was over rock, not rock climbing with ropes and gear, but very rocky terrain. One morning, as I forged forward, taking caution to watch my steps, to the top of Beech Mountain in Acadia, Maine, I kept hearing these words in my head, look back, look back. Let this be the topic for reflection, look back.

After about the 3rd or 4th calling I stopped and turned around. Incredible! The view of the path I was climbing with the trees turning color, the sunlight sifting through the leaves onto the path below, and the shadows formed by the rocks I had just climbed were as breath taking as the views I encountered from the tops of mountains and over cliffs on previous days. I was grateful that God had called me to look back because I could have missed it all.

Yet the call continued, look back, look back. I found myself almost annoyed that this message kept coming back into my head. After all I had looked back and I was trying to focus on the path ahead of me, it was steep and rocky and I did not want to lose my footing. I took a deep breath and turned to look back once more and there it was the real message I was supposed to receive. I was being called to see the people. The others I had come to know during our week together were making the journey, too. Our paths, our lives were being forever touched by this time together. We were sharing a similar experience in our own unique way, sharing joy, sharing laughter, sharing pain, sharing burdens. I was suddenly filled with gratitude for those on the journey with me.

Those on the journey with me? Yes, look back upon the journey and remember those who have been on the journey with me, those who have laughed with me, those who have cried with me, those who have helped me carry my burdens. There have been so many people in my life. Many of those people continue to be with me regularly. Many, however, were a part of my life for only a portion of the journey. Some of those people are no longer here to share the journey. But each individual has touched my life at just the right moment of my journey to afford me what it was I needed. In many cases I am probably not even aware of the reason why they were a part of my journey, but God knows. God places people in our path that can be for us his hands and feet, lifting us, walking with us.

Sometimes I hear people say, "don't look back, just keep looking forward". I agree with this statement to some degree. There are certainly things that happen to us in life, which we do not need to return to. Painful experiences can stop us from living life fully. There is, however, a purpose for looking back ever so briefly at the painful times in order for you to remember those who helped you through, remembering those who were there to lift you and to walk with you. If you never look back you risk missing some special people in your life. No matter how briefly their path intersected with yours or mine, they were there because God knew you and I needed them at that particular time. They are with you on the steep climb of life, which is sometimes rugged, winding, and exhausting just like climbing a mountain. Every person whether they journey with you today or have simply crossed your path in the past helps you become the person you are called to be.

Your spirit grows, strengthens, and matures with every encounter in life. If you fail to stop and look back, always looking ahead at the obstacles in your path, you miss the opportunity to thank those people along the way who have encouraged your climb. It is great to get to the top of the mountain and see the fabulous view, but don't miss out on the view along the way.

Questions to ponder:
Who are the people who have helped me make my journey?
Have I thanked them for what they have provided me?
How has God encouraged me to look back in gratitude?

In the Midst of Chaos

*Consider it pure joy, my brothers, whenever you face
trials of many kinds, because you know that the testing
of your faith develops perseverance. Perseverance must
finish its work so that you may be mature and complete,
not lacking anything. If any of you lacks wisdom, he
should ask God, who gives generously to all without finding fault, and it will be given to him. But when he asks,
he must believe and not doubt, because he who doubts is
like a wave of the sea, blown and tossed by the wind.*
—JAMES 1:2-6

It is good to be writing you this letter today. I have a grateful heart for my experiences in Africa a few weeks ago and a
new appreciation for my home in Reedsburg, Wisconsin, USA.
While I was gone there were many things happening in the
news here in the US regarding the economy and the stability
of our country. There seems to be a lot of focus on this subject.
May I reflect with you here on the topic of being in the midst
of chaos?

What does it mean for us to be experiencing this chaos in
our life? Is there a greater purpose in the events happening
around us? I trust there is. It will be up to each of us to discover
the true purpose of our situations, which is true of any chaotic
time in our life. I want to share with you a story that helped me
sort out the purpose.

While I was in Africa I had the opportunity to visit a school
for albino children and blind children. There is so much I could
say about this experience, but I will try to focus on one story.

This boarding school had 99 children, ages 8 to 14 and 40 beds. Some children slept 2 to a bed and those not in a bed slept on the concrete. There were no toys at the school, not even a ball, not one single toy. The children were clean, their beds were clean and the teacher there (who had attended as a blind student and returned to teach these children) was very kind and grateful to have us there; initially delivering malaria nets to cover the children's beds and then for our return visit delivering miscellaneous toys, matchbox cars, stuffed animals, jump ropes, balls, books, safari hats and more importantly 20 mattresses with the promise of 20 more to be delivered the following week.

We (the group of Rotarians I traveled with) distributed a safari hat and a toy to each child as they stood quietly in line, even to the point of causing us to wonder if they had ever played with toys before. We wondered if they knew what to do with them? As they continued to stand quietly in line wearing their safari hats and holding the toys in their hands we felt drawn to initiate play with the children, engaging them to play with one another. Before long there was a lovely song in the air, the song of children laughing. My heart was so lifted by this experience of bringing laughter into the lives of these children that day.

A group of us began talking about the day and as I turned around I saw a blind young man, probably 13 or 14 standing perfectly still in his place in the line that no longer existed with no one around him and somehow no toy in his hand. The other children all running and laughing and as I still picture the scene, there was chaos all around him and he was calmly standing in the midst of it. My heart broke and I fought the tears that wanted to come gushing forward. I went over to this young man and took his hand, spoke to him and led him to a group of boys playing with cars. I asked if they could show the cars to their friend and they happily did so. He began to interact with the other boys in the activity.

I noticed that my heart became angry about this situation. The disparity of the school, the fact that my grandchildren and so many children in the US have more toys than they can possibly play with and these children had none, but also at God for letting this young man live his life in darkness. I wondered, what was the purpose of this young man's life? How would he fulfill his purpose with such a disadvantaged life (seen through my eyes)?

Well the tears I felt for that young man continue to flow every time I tell this story, but no longer in wonder of his purpose, but rather in gratitude for all he showed me through his eyes. He demonstrated to me what I need to do in the chaos. I need to trust that God will intervene. This young man allowed God to reveal to me a depth of my own compassion that I was unaware of, the level of trust that can exist in chaos, and the level of gratitude that needs to be present in all circumstances.

We are likely to face some uncertainty and instability in our lives. Chaos might invade our life. You might think there is no comparison between the chaos of that day at the school and the chaos of the world you live in, but I disagree. I believe that in the midst of any kind of chaos if our spirit is as calm as that young man demonstrated our blindness will be removed and we will be able to see God in the midst of the chaos.

Questions to ponder:
What does chaos look like in my life?
How does God help me in my blindness to see his purpose?

Room with a View

෬෬

*The world is round and the place which may seem like
the end may also by only the beginning.*

IVY BAKER PRIEST

෬෬

As I traveled home from an incredible journey through an area, which up until recently I had only read about, I was encouraged to reflect on my experiences there. The scenes of my travels replayed in my mind. I do not wish to bore you with the details of my vacation, but rather to share with you the insight I gained in traveling from room to room in God's creation. Every room has a view of God's eternal love for us. Each room had something to offer my spirit.

The first stop on our journey through California was Redwood National Forest and upon entrance into the redwood grove utter silence was observed. I told my husband that the trees were 'so quiet'. He laughed. But, there in the forest those majestic trees demanded silence, allowing my spirit to absorb the view with no distractions from the outside world. My spirit was invited to look through the window of God's eyes. I saw the beauty of the creator. Every direction in this forest offered inspiration. I was standing in a room (of the earth) with a view. Every space of this earth is a room in God's creation and there is a view waiting to be noticed and it is full with vibrant life. Every detail, the tiniest flower, the delicate ferns and moss, and the streams of rushing water over grand rock formations, which have been so pleasantly placed to afford a rhythmic sound all contributing to the overall beauty of the view.

Along the trek through Sequoia National Park one of my favorite sequoias was titled "Room Tree". A tree room? I envisioned a hollow tree with a space to spread out and sleep. The "Room Tree" welcomed you in through a draped opening. Hollowed high it offered a spacious surrounding for my spirit to feel enveloped in security. Little did I imagine that within this hollow tree 20 feet above me would be a 40 foot skylight! That's right, looking up 20 feet there was an opening in the side of this tree that invited the sky into the room. I stood watching the blue clouds float by. I imagined a starlit night and the security this giant tree could provide (of course the reality is that I could get wet or have visitors through this incredible natural skylight, but that is not part of the reflection).

What can be said about the room in Yosemite National Park with its waterfalls and artistic rock formations? What of the room overlooking the Pacific Ocean with its crashing waves upon the jagged cliffs and the whales spouting in the distance? What of the room overlooking the vineyards, a reminder of the source to which I cling drawing nourishment for my thirsting spirit, a vine twisting and turning to support the stretching branch of my searching spirit?

The old adage to "stop and smell the roses" became a theme as we traveled through the countryside laden with rose bushes, but the phrase took on a much broader meaning than simply pausing to sniff flowers. It invited me to open my spirit to the room before me, the room with a view.

Although vision gives dimension to the view, our other senses contribute, as well. Our senses, the sense of smell, as you experience the aroma in the air, the sense of touch, while the breeze brushes against your skin, the sense of hearing, as you take in the sounds of the world around you, all enhance the scene, the experience. The sense of taste might even contribute as you taste the humidity or the raindrops on your tongue. Each of our senses provides us with a new way to experience our surroundings. I have come to believe, however, that it is our sense of *faith* that makes the view magnificent. In the words of an old hymn, by Henry Alford, we are reminded of the power of this sense, "We walk by faith and not by sight, no gracious words we hear from him who spoke as none e'er spoke; but we believe him near".

Here at home there is inspiration, too. God calls me to appreciate the room I am in at any given time, not only on vacation, but also in the daily-ness of life. God is writing to you in your room with a view and your faith will allow you to receive your message from the creator. Your spirit waits. I encourage you to take it all in, every detail.

Questions to ponder:
How do my senses experience my room?
What is the view from my daily life?
Where has it been difficult to see the view
God has offered me?

& Beyond

♆♆

You, my brothers, were called to be free. But do not use your freedom to indulge the sinful nature; rather, serve one another in love. —GALATIANS 5: 13

♆♆

In the spring of 2011, my husband and I traveled to South Africa. On the last 4 days of our vacation we toured with a company by the name of "& Beyond". The logo had a soaring bird with the symbol "&" and the word "Beyond" directly below it. One day after our trip I was walking and I realized a connection between the name and my adventures in South Africa. I realized how deeply it touched my spirit. Let me share my reflection with you.

This trip was wonderful beyond my expectations. At every turn there were people offering to assist us whether it be to carry bags, offer us a refreshing glass of juice, offer a cool towel after traveling a long distance or to show me how to use the computer to send a message home, the people of South Africa represented hospitality beyond my expectations, and then there were the accommodations. Here again, I was more surprised with each place we stayed. The rooms were decorated with pristine white comforters and colorful accent pillows. Many of our meals were served outside and the food was prepared and served with great attention to detail. The staff placed the silverware and stemware in precise locations around tables, carried food and beverages long distances and served foods that were exquisite in their presentation, beyond my expectations.

The last place we stayed was to be a "thatched roof hut". I expected a 10 foot square hut with a thatched roof. The reality was a round hut approximately 25 feet in diameter with a quaint front porch and French doors that opened to a bedroom decorated with a pure white comforter, a white coverlet, and sheer white princess style drape as the headboard! Was I really in the bush country of South Africa? Stay with me now, I am getting to the point. From my previous trip to Tanzania I know there are many differences in accommodations on safari and clearly we were on a trip that chose not to rough it, but without these surprises around every corner I think I would have missed the message being sent.

When I would comment on how much extra work it was for the staff to prepare outdoor meals, keep pure white linens pure white in the dusty bush country, or any number of other things, my husband would say to me, "it is their job". I would have to agree with him that it was their job, but it was the way in which they did their job that zeroed in on the true nature of "& Beyond".

The smiles on their faces would not have had to be there. You cannot pay people to smile sincere smiles and you know when someone is smiling sincerely. The smiles on their faces showed me that they place their hopes and dreams in something bigger than the paycheck at the end of the week and you can believe me their paycheck is far from great. They represented a zest for life that seems to be missing in many areas of the world in which we live.

There was a sense of joy in their lives that is perhaps lost to some degree here at home, in this state, in this country. Life in some ways has become too serious, too focused on money and power. The people of South Africa sang, danced, and laughed while doing their work and daily activities. Even those living in desolate areas were dressed in clean clothes, polished shoes and wore smiles on their faces as they waved to us cheerfully.

I know I experience more joy when I allow each encounter with another person, each adventure to be as pure and free from expectations as a white comforter, when I allow each experience to be written on the blank sheet of a new day, and when I allow myself to be grateful each evening at sunset for the day just the way it played out.

Our trip ended with "& Beyond" so that I could realize the hope that lies within the soaring spirit willing to raise me up "& Beyond" the limited hope of my humanness. Let your spirit soar with a hope that takes you "& Beyond".

Questions to ponder:
Do I expect too much?
Do I put too much emphasis on having
my expectations met?
Do my greatest disappointments come from
unmet expectations?

CHAPTER 9

Readiness

*Family and friends are gifts to the end
Memories shared are there to defend
The end*

The Message to Get Ready

৶৶

The definitive voice in the universe is Jesus. He is not one among many voices; his is the one voice over all voices.
—MAX LUCADO

৶৶

November is what I consider to be an in between month. Between fall and winter, like March is between winter and spring. The month of November holds many messages for us. Fluctuating temperatures and snowfalls sprinkled with days of warm sunshine are hints of the upcoming season. As winter fast approaches November allows us days to finish the harvest, cover the flower gardens, and ready our homes for winter. Are you getting ready? There is something more important to prepare for than winter. I want to share with you this month some thoughts on the messages all around us and the way we do or do not respond to them in preparing to be ready.

Think of all the ways we receive messages. We hear, I will send you an email, I will drop you a line, I will give you a call, or I will leave a note. We say things like, call my cell phone and just leave it on my answering machine, I'll get it later. Put a note on the counter before you leave. I will check my emails first thing in the morning. We are constantly sending and receiving messages. We use these messaging options for important messages. Everything from grocery items we forgot to pick up, to confirming doctor's appointments. I have been known to leave myself a message on the answering machine as a reminder to do something when I get home or to the office. But there are bigger messages that I want to reflect on in this writing.

Beyond the messages in the changing of the seasons, beyond the messages we send to one another, are there messages that we continue to receive and fail to acknowledge, ignore, or pretend that we don't hear? I think there are. All too often I think we forget the messages of love that God sends to us. God loves us the way we are. God has created us in his own image. God will not leave us. We are precious in God's eyes. We are his children. God calls us each by name. God will take us home. Messages of the greatest love I can imagine come into our lives every day, at anytime of the day. They can touch our spirit deeply. These messages allow you to strengthen your relationship with God.

What about the other messages? Events like natural disasters, crime, violence, and personal loss all hold messages for us, too. They remind us that life is precious, life is unpredictable, life is too short, life is unfair, and that life is a mystery. How do we respond to these messages? They certainly require more than a mental note to pick up milk at the grocery store. They require us to pause and reflect on our own lives, our families, our relationships, and our communities. Beyond that they call us to reflect on our own personal relationship with God. They are messages of readiness.

Over the past couple of months I have had conversations with individuals who have made comments about not knowing what the world is coming to. There have been expressions of fear, helplessness, and hopelessness in response to the events that occur in the news every day. These responses seem to repeat themselves. I had young woman ask me in the fall before the new millennium, what if the world ends on January 1st 2000. My response was this, what if the world ends tomorrow? What would you do differently knowing that the world was coming to an end? The fact is we do not know when the end of our earthly life will come. This message seems to be forgotten or overlooked sometimes. We rush into life as though we have plenty of time to get ready.

Ready as you may be for the winter to set in, how ready are you for the coming of our Lord? I often remind myself that the work I most need to do is in preparation for this upcoming event, the coming of the Lord. I use the messages all around me as reminders of what the priorities in life are or should be. Like the many missed messages of this culture, I too miss many of God's daily messages. The ones I get I hang on to with great faith that God loves me and is always with me. I believe he wants each of you to receive this message directly from him through prayer and reflection of the world around you.

Messages are sent to us every day. Day after day. At all times of the day. God whispers to us his saving grace. Listen for spiritual messages 24-7.

Questions to ponder:
Am I tuned in to receive God's messages?
When is my best time for communicating with God?

The Final Chapter

There is a time for everything, and a season for every activity under heaven: a time to be born and a time to die.
—*ECCLESIASTES 3:1-2*

One year in early June I had an opportunity to attend a conference in La Crosse, WI, which is one of my favorite areas of the state. The beauty of the marsh, the river, and the bluffs created a reflective environment for this conference on death, dying and bereavement. I realize this would not be a topic most people would seek to read about, but I encourage you to stay with me in this reflection as it does apply to everyone. I want to share with you one of the messages from this conference.

One evening during our conference we were invited to watch a documentary entitled, "Facing Death". This film had aired on Public Television in the fall of 2010. Perhaps some of you have seen it (if not, I imagine you could "Google" it). At any rate it was an extremely thought provoking documentary highlighting the choices we or our families might face in the last months, weeks and days of life.

That night I awoke with this thought, 'To Die or Not to Die—That Is <u>Not</u> The Question!' The reality is I will die. We *all* die. The question is *How?* Many of you have lost loved ones suddenly and in one second your life was changed forever. Many of you have lost loved ones to long hard battles with chronic or fatal illness and your life too was changed forever. Death comes to each of us. Is there a way to defray some of the suffering that occurs during the dying process or after someone dies by talking about the reality prior to death? I believe there is. We can live our lives as if we are going to die because we will. We can plan to have a final chapter in our life because we will.

Let me propose making a plan. When a woman is going to have a baby she and her doctor talk about a "birth plan". Why not talk about a "when I am dying plan"? The documentary suggested that 80% of us will die under the care of a healthcare professional (in a hospital or nursing home setting) and I have heard this statistic before. If that is true then 80% of us have time to make a "when I am dying plan". After seeing this documentary I believe it is critical that we start looking at dying and death from the mindset of planning. The stumbling block in this is none of us think this statistic applies to us.

When will we get to the final chapter of our life? An unpredictable question. Will we know when we are in the final chapter of life? A difficult question. It is quite likely that we will not know right away. What will we do if and when we come to that realization? Based on my experience there are a number of reactions to this question. Everything from denying the reality to embracing it. What will our family do? This question is easy to answer. In the absence of planning, family members will struggle with not knowing what to do and there will likely be arguments between family members about what to do.

We live in a world of great technology. It certainly has its benefits and many people are living full lives today as a result of that technology. It may be part of our story in the future. But the reality is in the absence of a plan or direction in what our values and beliefs are regarding death and dying many of us will given medical interventions that we would prefer to not have because our families will not know what else to do. The documentary was extremely sad to me in that no one ever talked with the patients or their families about their fears, their grief, or the support available to help them to help them embrace this process and make good days for their loved one in their final chapter on this earth. Talk with your family, friends and your doctor about your choices. You can decide whether you want to spend the last months, days or hours of your life running to doctor's appointments or whether you might rather spend the time visiting with family and friends, telling stories, hearing stories, laughing and crying over the life you have shared together.

We trust that God is with us throughout our living and our dying. We read in Ecclesiastes 3:1-2, "There is a time for everything, and a season for every activity under heaven: a time to be born and a time to die". When a baby is ready to come there is no stopping it. Nature takes its course and the woman is supported in labor with comfort measures and encouraging words. When death comes, I believe, we have the opportunity to allow nature to take its course and provide comfort measures and encouraging words to our loved ones.

When I reach the final chapter of my life and my body begins to die, I pray that my family and friends will support me in my journey with their presence and love and not hold onto my lifeless body with medical equipment. I pray that they will release me so that I might go to my Heavenly Father who waits for me, and each one of you, to be with him in eternity.

Questions to ponder:
What would I want in the final chapter of my life?
Who should I talk with about my wishes?

Focus

୨୧

Wherever your treasure is, there your heart and thoughts will also be. —MATTHEW 6:21

୨୧

One day, as my husband and I ate breakfast, we noticed a female cardinal in the birch tree outside our sun porch window. Only the night before at supper we watched a male cardinal swoop from the birch tree to a small hydrangea tree located close to the house. We began to wonder if there indeed was a nest in the tree (although at first glance the night before we found nothing). Now with this new clue we looked a little closer. We took the time to *focus.*

Sure enough with the naked eye we could see there were twigs arranged in the shape of a nest. We could hear a tiny chirping sound, yet we could not see a baby bird. My husband went for the binoculars. He brought the strongest pair we own. They did not work. The nest was too close for the high powered lenses. Granted these binoculars can see things far away amazingly well, but they were no good to us for this up-close discovery.

I sent him off to get the other, older, less "new and improved" binoculars. Now we could see the nest much more clearly, but there were still too many branches to see what was inside. I decided to pause, stand really still and focus on the nest. There it was. Movement. There was indeed a pulsation in the nest. I could not make out the features of the baby bird, but I could see the pulsation of life flowing within it.

It made me wonder. How focused was I on the pulsation of my life? You see, only days earlier, while I was out walking, the topic of staying focused came to mind as a great reflection for this time of my life when there seemed to be so many distractions. Even within the first minutes of considering the topic of staying focused on the present I was distracted by some event in the future. Then I was distracted by the cars going by. I was distracted by the smell of new asphalt. I was distracted into thinking that my topic for reflection should be distractions!

I did not do any writing that day. I was *too distracted*. I was *not focusing*! So God sent me yet another reminder for what he wanted me to hear. He sent me a tiny bird that beckoned me to focus on the pulsation of life not only in a tiny unseen bird, but also within myself.

I had been longing for weeks to focus on one thing at a time. Life was getting out of focus for me. I was constantly thinking about what I needed to do weeks down the road and how fast the time was going. I was constantly planning ahead. The pulse of my spirit was straining to stay the pace. I needed to focus on the here and now, on refueling my spirit.

These two events came to me just as I was approaching a day with nothing on the schedule! Nothing! No obligations, nothing needing to be done. Chores were completed to a point where a break was easily accepted. Enter in a full moon and the stage was set to *focus*!

Sometimes our binoculars are too high powered. We look at life in the distance. We focus on what is to come rather than what is in the here and now. Other times we try to see things through our own eyes and the distractions of life get in the way. They block our view. When we use the right lens, God's eyes, to view life we can see the very pulse of life.

When I view my life through God's eyes I can focus on what is really important in my life. I become more appreciative of what I have. I am better equipped to share his message with others. You may think it is the distractions of life that need to be dealt with, but let me encourage you the distractions of life will lose their power when you begin to *focus*.

Questions to ponder:
Does this verse also apply to where my focus is?
Will my heart and thoughts be where my focus is?
Where is my focus right now?
Which lens am I using in my life, a high powered lens, my own vision, or God's eyes?

What's the Secret?

၅၃

Here is a hint. You will not find the secret on a shelf!

၅၃

It is summer! When summer is in full swing I imagine you have opportunities to be with family. Family gatherings give us all the chance to talk with our eldest relatives and ask them what their secret is. Ah, the secret to long life. We most likely share with them what we are doing to achieve the same goal. I would like to reflect with you on this topic of life and living and this question, what's the secret?

Being in the healthcare field since 1985 I have had many conversations with physicians, specialists, staff, patients, and family members about how to stay healthy and live a long life. In fact, there have been people throughout history who have claimed to have discovered the secret of life. It would seem as though it is something we all have in common, a search for the secret to living a long life. I have found there are several ideas about this secret, here are a few I have been introduced to or reminded of recently.

Vinegar. You know I think vinegar might be the answer. I know people who claim that an ounce of apple cider vinegar daily will cure whatever ails you and for many of those people I believe it does help them feel better. For others the idea of drinking straight vinegar *causes* them to be ill (that would be me!).

Keifer grains. Keifer grains are used to make a probiotic drink that will keep your gut healthy and I have family members who faithfully drink this beverage daily and it does seem to be providing them with stomach stability. I on the other hand cannot get past the thought of drinking a combination of ingredients that includes milk at room temperature for 24 hours (come to think of it though, my stomach is better just resisting the need to drink something like that!).

Vitamin D. Omega 3 and Fish Oil. Lots of water. Whole grains and fiber. It seems as though there are as many ideas about what is best for us as there are people. I had a conversation with 2 of my sister-in-laws and they were discussing the approaches they were taking to stay healthy and live a long life. They teased me when I openly resisted all of them. I told them that when people ask me at age 110 what my secret was I would declare that it was because I have never taken a supplement for longer than 1 week. We all laughed.

I do not mean to pooh pooh any of this. Clearly there is research and practical application for using many of these healthy lifestyle choices. But it made me think and I wondered if I have ever heard anyone say anything about the benefits of spiritual connectedness in living a long life. Furthermore, is it really a long life we want to live or is a deep, rich life most important?

I love it when a simple conversation that leads to laughter causes me to think deeper about any given topic. Is it what we do for our bodies that is the secret to living or is it what we do for others? Is it rather feeding others that feeds our soul with life giving sustenance? These words from John 6:35, "I am the Bread of Life" and from Matthew 11:28, "Come to me, all you who are weary and burdened and I will give you rest" came to my mind. Words of strength and support nurturing my spirit and assuring me that my spiritual connectedness is a key ingredient to living fully the life I have been given.

I have had to stop and think about whether I give as much attention to my spiritual food as I do the food for my flesh. I would have to admit that there is not a perfect balance here. I spend far more time thinking about what goes into my mouth than what goes into my heart. Only time with God will fill my heart space and I am with God every time I am with another person for God resides in us all.

Ah ha, there it is! The Secret! Spending time with others, being with others, serving others increases my time with God and deepens my spiritual connectedness. Regardless of the length of my life I will live a deeper richer life if I am in relationship with others. In fact, I am going to claim this as *The Secret* and try to spend more time in relationship than in the supplement aisle.

Questions to ponder:
Have I thought about what might be the
secret to a long life?
How do relationships impact one's life?
How can I find balance for living life fully?

Trapped Inside

ՉՉ

We can deal with the ambulance if God is in it. We can stomach the ICU if God is in it. We can face the empty house if God is in it. He is. —MAX LUCADO

ՉՉ

Winter was upon us and as many of you know I love to find beauty in the snow and crisp air, but the first thing on my mind on this particular morning was the fact that I could not walk outside. I had been walking inside all week and for another day it looked as though I was going to be trapped inside. The country roads were covered with ice and it was too risky to walk outside for fear of falling or having a car slide off the road into my path. So I prepared to accept the fact that I would be once again, trapped inside. I started to think about not only being trapped physically, but also about what it means to be trapped spiritually. There is more.

Later that morning I went to visit a woman with a friend of mine. As we arrived, by phone, we discovered that she was unable to navigate the stairs and had resigned that she would be unable to visit with us. After assuring her that we would come to her, she invited us to use the back staircase where she would then let us in. As we approached the door we could hear her working the key in the lock. We tried the screen door, but it was also locked. It appeared as though she was trapped inside. Questions began to go through my mind. What if she needed help? There was no way for us to get in. Or, what if she needed to get out for a fire? She seemed, to me, in all estimation to be trapped inside. Again I wondered what it must be like for her spiritually to be unable to come and go as she pleased (let me clarify for those of you wondering about her well-being, she does have a caregiver and family, there are other ways into the apartment, there are systems in place for her to have help and she utilizes those systems as needed).

I began to wonder why these circumstances presented themselves on the same day only hours apart. I was about to find out. As my friend and I prayed silently for her to get the lock unlocked her son arrived and directed us into the home and to his mother's apartment. As we entered her room she was so delighted to see my friend. Her biggest concern was not that she could not get the door open to freedom, but rather that our time to visit might run out before she got the door open. She invited us to stay and we sat with her happy to now be in her smiling presence.

As I watched her interact with my friend I found myself marveling at the peace that pervaded her whole being. As she shared her adjustments to her new limitations at this stage of her life she sprinkled her conversation with gratitude for her strong spiritual connection and the blessing of friends and gentle spirits in her life, like the one sitting at her side. As we prepared to leave, I hugged her and asked for God's peace to be upon her and a big smile crossed her face and she joyfully chimed in, "Yes, yes, isn't that just it, when we find God's peace we have everything".

Faced with the prospect of a long winter and likely many days of having to be inside, I am preparing to search out God's peace and I want to encourage you to search for God's peace in your life. Drawing on a personal relationship will afford you and me freedom from feeling trapped physically or spiritually. I will hold on to his words found in, Isaiah 26:3, "You will keep in perfect peace all who trust in you, whose thoughts are fixed on you", Psalm 34:4-5, "I prayed to the Lord, and he answered me, freeing me from all my fears. Those who look to him for help will be radiant with joy" and Psalm 34:17-18, "The Lord hears his people when they call to him for help. He rescues them from all their troubles. The Lord is close to the brokenhearted; he rescues those who are crushed in spirit".

Let us hold on to the promise of inner peace in those times when we feel trapped inside, for I know we are not alone, we are not trapped inside, and when we seek and find God's peace we will one day have "everything".

Questions to ponder:
Have I ever felt trapped inside?
Have I experienced God's peace in my life?
How can I share a sense of peace with others?

Time is Running Out

❦

Let us not become weary in doing good, for at the proper
time we will reap a harvest if we do not give up. There-
fore, as we have opportunity, let us do
good to all people... —GALATIANS 6:9-10

❦

I was thinking about having to write another reflection and asking God to please hurry and send me a topic for reflection because time was running out for me to submit my writing. I had just one week to complete my reflection and the days ahead were looking pretty full. Yesterday I still had nothing, or so I thought. In actuality I had the topic last week, but I guess I needed a couple more clues and they came through the weather and the media! Let me reflect with you about this topic as time is indeed running out.

It had been an awesome fall for outdoor activities and although the calendar predicted that winter would be upon us soon, the weather continued to distract us from this reality. There are things we must do before winter sets in. The farmers have been busy taking advantage of the warm, dry days for bringing in the harvest. The flowers are shutting down for a winter's rest. We know that we should bring in the outdoor furniture one of these days, but not just yet, it is too nice out, surely there will be another day. Then when that first snowfall hits and the temperatures drop we wish we would have taken the time to put things away when we did not have to bundle up and sweep the snow off the furniture in order to pull the pieces inside. Oh, how easily we are lured away from the reality that time is running out!

Time is running out! Only two days left! Don't miss this opportunity! These are a few of the slogans companies use to persuade us to spend money and they insist we do it quickly. Could they also be applied to the way we should live our lives?

Let's think about the connection between my not knowing when God would send me a message, the distractions in life and the urgency with which we should act upon this truth--for each of us time is running out. The clincher is, however, that we do not have a seasonal calendar that helps us predict and prepare for when our time will run out. Indeed, the consequences for running out of time before we do what we need to do will be far greater than being cold and miserable. The consequences of our failures to complete the tasks before us will have a lasting effect on those we leave behind.

What if time runs out after you cut someone off in traffic, after you yell at your spouse or your children, after you refuse to make eye contact with the clerk behind the counter because you are busy talking on your cell phone? Each day we have the chance to show kindness, to be considerate toward the people around us, whether they are family members, friends, colleagues or strangers. Being kind and considerate can provide life lessons for generations to come. Such simple gestures can make a world of difference and a difference in the world!

Simple gestures of kindness, consideration, politeness, smiling, shaking hands, and saying thank you can lift the spirit of someone else and the bonus is that these gestures can lift your spirit as well. So shake off the anger, resentment, and feelings of frustration. Extend forgiveness. Seek forgiveness. I encourage you to practice using your time to spend lavishly the fruit of the spirit found within, which as we learn in Galatians 5:22 is, love, joy, peace, patience, kindness, faithfulness, gentleness and self-control". I know of no negative consequences for these actions toward others.

The month of November as the days grow shorter and the wind becomes colder; reflect on the ways you can ensure that time will not run out before you have had a chance to touch the life of someone else in a way that will have a positive lasting impact on their future and likewise their actions toward others. You can make a difference in someone's world, but don't put it off because with each day we are closer to time running out.

Questions to ponder:
How am I being distracted from the truth that
time is running out?
What lasting impact will my gestures have?

CHAPTER 10

Reflections from the Christmas and New Year's Season

୧୧

My Christmas Prayer

*Heavenly Father, guide me this season to remember the reason,
the reason we celebrate, the special gift you sent us
May I remember the purpose of my life is not to supply my
family and friends with material possessions, but to share my
heart
openly with them. Fill my heart with joy, Lord, that I might
share heart gifts freely with my loved ones. May the
compassionate heart of Jesus live within me this season and
always. Amen.*

It's the Most Wonderful Time of the Year?

For God so loved the world that he gave his one and only Son, that whoever believes in him shall not perish but have eternal life. —JOHN 3:16

Once again, it is upon us. The season we promote as being the most wonderful. I am writing in mid-November and I have noticed people seem to be in frenzy, putting their Christmas decorations up. It seems as though this preparation starts earlier every year and what is the reason? Are we living in an illusion that if we decorate for the Christmas season that all will be wonderful, everything will glisten, fragrances will be satisfying, and hearts will be warm by the fire? The display may be fabulous, but what makes it so wonderful? Thus, the reason I have placed a question mark in the title of this reflection.

One day the famous Christmas song, *It's the Most Wonderful Time of the Year*, by Andy Williams came into my head and as I started singing it the words changed to 'it's the most challenging time of the year', not sure why but they did. Over and over they repeated in my mind and I simply had to open my heart to the message being sent to share with you regarding this time of the year.

Often, when I am shopping, I am drawn to whatever it is that supports the items being sold, like a sled piled high with winter sweaters or the pie cupboard hanging full of candles and most of the time when I inquire about the cost of the item I am told that it is "for display only". Sleds no longer used for sledding, pie cupboards no longer filled with delicious pies seem to have lost their purpose and have become valuable only on display. Ask yourself these questions, am I being used for my purpose, am I mirroring the face of Christ to others, what was the reason Jesus came to be with us, am I with others in the same way? Ask yourself this question, "Am I for display only"?

I cannot say that I quickly answered any of these questions, but the last one really required a deep look into my own heart. I found some spots covered with tinsel. There were lights on but the glare made it seem not so clear. Perhaps I would like to think I am fulfilling my purpose, but I really had to stop and consider that question, am I for display only, and is there a connection between my purpose and my actions? It may seem as though I have drifted from my original reflection topic, but I will make the connection I promise (I think).

For many, many people the Christmas season is not the most wonderful time of the year. Many grieve the loss of a loved one and it may be their first Christmas without them or it may be their 10th Christmas without them, but they remember their loss, their longing. Economic challenges are everywhere. Hours have been cut, jobs have been lost and families have had to cut back severely. There are families separated by harsh words spoken even years ago that cannot reconcile and for them this time of the year is truly an effort in fulfilling an obligation to spend time together. And in a world that thinks we need to start earlier and earlier to get our displays in order we are lengthening the challenges these individuals face.

Well then what is it, wonderful or challenging? More importantly, what is my role, your role, in reconciling these truths; there is joy in celebrating the birth of a Savior sent to save the world and there is pain when someone's world is falling apart. To begin, we must remember we too have a purpose on this earth. We must carry out the purpose for which we were designed. We must remember that we are to love one another, to serve one another, to carry one another's burdens.

During the Christmas season the call for us to be more than "for display only" is stronger than ever. It will be our reaching out and lifting up those experiencing great challenges in their lives that will reconcile the two. You and I have the potential to make it the most wonderful time of the year by coming together in one spirit of love to ensure that those around us are supported throughout this season and the next.

Questions to ponder:
What challenges do I experience during the holidays?
How can I make the holidays a little easier for someone else?

Give Him a Room

ℒℒ

Make a manger for the Savior of your soul. Give him a
room and he will love and make you whole.
—KATHY MCGOVERN

ℒℒ

One morning as I rose for the day and began reviewing my schedule I found an activity I truly wanted to do being pushed to the bottom of the list because I did not seem to have room in my day to allow it to happen. Yet it wanted to be there on my list. It wanted room in my life. Having the room or making the room let this be the topic for our reflection.

It is back, that time of year when we scurry around trying to find room in our schedules for a number of activities. We try to find room in our schedules to go shopping, to bake cookies and treats, to wrap presents, to accommodate extra guests, to attend Christmas parties and to send out Christmas cards. If we stop and think about it this time of the year can be a crazy time for many people. For me it has become a time to intentionally stop and reflect on the importance of the activities I choose to do.

The first question I ask is this, 'is it going to make a difference in someone's life', and then, 'is it going to matter in the big scheme of things'? This morning I was encouraged to ask these questions in regard to the room in my schedule. The answer became obvious when I was called to reflect on this word room. Do I have room? Have I made room? Will I make room? Is there room in my heart for what matters most? I paused in my decision making process to check in with my spirit and ask God what I should do. Believe it or not the debate was over finishing a project or visiting a friend who is ill. Yes, I know, this should be a no-brainer. The most valuable thing, the thing that will matter to me in the long run is to visit my friend. Haven't we all experienced the frailty of life? Do I know if my friend will be with me when I finish my project? The choice became so easy when I looked at it from God's perspective. What matters most are relationships and the bottom line is this we do not know how long we will be in relationship with another.

Here we are again, however, immersed in the commercialization of an event in history, which offers us wholeness, rushing around as if it has lost its true meaning. There is a line in my favorite Christmas song written by Kathy McGovern in 1976, a woman from Arizona whom I never had a chance to meet. Her song had become a favorite for the members of St. Elizabeth Ann Seaton in Tuscan and I heard it for the first time in 1984. She wrote what has become for me the most beautiful story about the coming of our savior. In the third verse she writes, "Make a manger for the Savior of your soul. Give him a room and he will love and make you whole". This is such a powerful message for us all. Prepare. Yes, we must prepare. When we have prepared a room in our heart for Jesus to live we are made whole.

Here is the next challenge. Jesus does not want to simply come and visit you this Christmas. The Holy Spirit wants permanent residence in your heart. He is not asking for an overnight stay. He is asking for a lifetime relationship. Day in and day out he wants to live in your heart and be there for consultation, support, healing, gratitude, and celebration.

With our minds racing trying to figure out how we will make room in our schedules to finish all of the extra things we feel we need to do in this 30 day span of time and our bodies trying to maintain the energy needed to accomplish these extra tasks we often overlook the needs of our spirit. We may have made room in our hearts long ago for Jesus to live, but for some reason we forget to consult him about the urgency of certain activities over others. I was reminded today of the great and loving consult that resides in my heart. And I am grateful when he knocks loud enough for me to remember his presence when life gets so loud I forget. Today my project will have to wait, my friend will not.

Questions to ponder:
What's on my list?
Where is my priority today?
Have I made a room for Jesus to reside in my heart?

In the Darkness of Night

✑✑

If I say, "Surely the darkness will hide me and the light
become night around me," even the darkness will not be
dark to you; the night will shine like the day, for darkness
is as light to you. —PSALM 139:11

✑✑

The morning air is crisp and smells like winter as I ponder the message that has been long in coming. Today in the darkness of night God has given clarity to a message that began last winter. Now is the time for me to share it with you.

One moon light night last winter I was encouraged to pull myself out of bed and go for a walk. First, understand that I am not easily aroused at 4:30 a.m., which still constitutes nighttime in the dead of winter, but this particular night the moon was so bright I could not imagine rolling over and going back to sleep. The night sky was incredible, a black backdrop enhanced the sparkling stars and a brilliant full moon caused the snow to glisten with diamonds. Breathtaking! As I walked I thanked God for the beauty of this winter's night and then, I noticed shadows, shadows in the darkness. There was so much light in the darkness that shadows existed. There had to be a message here, but what was it. I sat with it, reflected on it, jotted down notes about it, but nothing became of it. I put it aside as simply a pleasurable walk with God.

In March of 2008 I experienced a personal darkness in the loss of my brother-in-law. Over the year I have shared many tears with others experiencing their own personal darkness. Our community suffered deep darkness in the June floods. In September I traveled to Africa. There I experienced the darkness of poverty. In the last months of that year, we as a nation have experienced darkness in our sliding economy and many individuals have experienced the darkness of job losses.

So today once again walking in the darkness before sunrise, I am thinking about the Christmas season, reflecting on the darkness and then it hit me. The message God started last winter and shared with me throughout this past year gained clarity in the darkness. Jesus was born in the darkness of night. Jesus comes to us in our darkness. Jesus is present around the world and this time; this season is perfectly placed for us to focus on what we really need in darkness, the Light of a Savior.

Last winter the light casting shadows was the light of Christ guarding my way as I walked. Even when I could not see what was in the shadows, I could keep my focus on the light and not be afraid. As the shadows entered my heart when my brother-in-law died it was the light of Christ that kept me from closing down to fear. As I watched others deal with the loss of their home in the flood many shared their faith in Jesus Christ as their stronghold. Others who mourn the loss of a loved one share openly their trust in the Lord not knowing what they would do if they did not have Jesus in their life. A young man in Africa shared with me the presence of God in the midst of chaos by exhibiting a calm spirit.

In the darkness of night, when we are burdened or afraid, Jesus Christ brings us hope. He is the light we can count on to add clarity to our lives. But you see the message was not revealed all at once. The reasons for our losses and burdens will likely not be cleared up all at once either. The shadows of night will no doubt be there from time to time, but the light of Christ will light our way through the darkness. Over time there may be some clarity to our experiences. The shadows in my life may not be removed, but my path will become clear enough for me to make my way guided by the light that comes in the darkness of night, the light of a Savior.

Questions to ponder:
Do I fear the shadows of night?
How has the light of the Savior lead me through dark times?

Be the light

∂∾

For to us a child is born, to us a son is given, and the government will be on his shoulders. And he will be called Wonderful Counselor, Mighty God, Everlasting Father, Prince of Peace. ISAIAH 9:6

∂∾

One morning I found myself being pulled from my bed by a soft light through the blinds. The time was 5:17 a.m. We had just turned back the clocks so it was no longer daylight savings time and I remember thinking how nice it was going be to have light so early again. Even though it was early (for me) I felt rested and decided to get up and walk. As I strolled into the kitchen and announced I was going out for a walk, my husband asked, "right away?" and I responded, "Yes". He pointed out the kitchen window and reminded me that it would be dark for a while yet. Yes indeed as I looked out the kitchen window toward the east there was no sign of the sun. I want to reflect with you this month about being called to be the light.

I decided to go out anyway trusting that God wanted me to walk this early. I grabbed my flashlight and my reflective vest and out the door I went. As I rounded the corner of our garage there it was a brilliant light shining across the fields, the light of a harvest moon. I smiled to myself and thanked God for this amazing reminder of his presence in my life. But as I continued to walk and pray I discovered an even deeper message being sent by the light of the moon.

The message was this; each of us is called to be the light. The moon and stars do not only provide light in the darkness they tell us about the infinite light of Christ. We know when we see the moon and stars that there is a sun and that it will shine brightly in our lives once again. The sun never leaves us. Likewise the Son never leaves us. God is with us at all times and sometimes we are to be a reminder, the moon and stars, for someone else. We are to be a reminder to them that God has not left them, that God is with them even in their darkness and that once again brightness will fill their life.

Let me further explain how God shared this message with me. I was feeling somewhat melancholy that morning and praying for God to help me regain my joy that was for some reason slightly darkened. As I prayed the light of the moon reflected on the road lighting my way. As I turned my back toward the moon there was a little less light on the road but more light in my heart as I realized God's presence within lighting my path. I turned to acknowledge the moon and it had become somewhat dull. The intense brightness of the moon was no longer needed. My prayers were being answered and the Son was shining brightly from within again. I was reminded of the light Christ places within us to shine in our darkness. Sometimes I forget. I get too busy doing what I think I should do and then the world becomes dark. The moon's light nudged me back toward the light within toward the path God was lighting for me.

What do I mean when I say each of us is called to be the light? Consider if you would that during the holidays there are many people who do not feel like celebrating. The stresses of their world shadow the light. Darkness seems to fill their hearts and we are called to be the moon and stars for them shining as a reminder that Christ is with them even if it appears otherwise. If they can see the light of Christ in us they will remember that God's light is burning within them. We can illuminate their path and encourage them to trust that the light of Christ will shine brightly in their lives and lead them once again. Just as the sun will rise out of the darkness, the Son will rise within each of us in times of darkness.

I encourage you to *Be the Light* for someone else. May the light of Christ shine from your face upon someone today so that they will trust that the Son will shine again in their heart.

Questions to ponder:
Who has been the Light of Christ for my in
times of darkness?
For whom can I be the Light of Christ?

Heart Gifts

๛

Thanks be to God for his indescribable gift!
—*2 CORINTHIANS 9:15*

๛

The Christmas season is supposed to be a season of reflection, compassion, reaching out to others, and sharing our blessings. Unfortunately, I see this season for many people being a season of stress, frustration, financial strain and worry. Stress as they try to attend multiple gatherings in a couple of days. Worry as they try to find the perfect gift for a loved one. Frustration as they untangle the Christmas lights or fight the crowded shopping malls. Financial strain as they stretch their budget in an effort to give gifts to everyone on their list, plus the mailman! (Not that the mailman doesn't deserve a gift).

Each year as Christmas approaches I become more intent on helping others see the value of heart gifts. What is a heart gift? A heart gift is the most valuable gift you can give or receive. I realize this is my opinion, but again this year I wish to make it the opinion of others. How can I help others realize that the most precious gift you can give or receive comes from the heart and not from the wallet? I will share my insights with you. Then I ask you to reflect on your own experiences with heart gifts.

Once as chairman of the Wisconsin Parish Nurse Coalition I was given a gift. I certainly was not expecting a gift. The surprise was a welcomed feeling in my heart. But, the true surprise and even more welcome feeling came with the discovery of the kind of gift the package held. It was a heart gift, a beautiful prayer shawl, and what made it precious was not the deep plum color, soft texture, gentle warmth or delicate weave, but rather the love with which it was made. The creation of this shawl came from the heart. It was knit together in prayer and meditation for the one who was to receive it. This shawl was made for me by someone who offered me up in prayer. That is an awesome gift. When I wrap myself in it I feel the tenderness of the one whom put her heart into its creation.

Over the years I have had many gifts of the heart given to me by my family. The end result being precious in and of itself, but the true value of the gift being much deeper as it was the time, effort and heart that were given in addition to the end product. The process of planning and creating is what gives the gift depth and meaning.

What do you need in your life, more material stuff or more heart stuff? Gifts of true value do not have a dollar sign attached to them. You simply cannot put a price on gifts of the heart. Many of you might be cringing at the thought of foregoing the Christmas Wish List and giving a gift from the heart. You may wonder how your family will react. How will the kids survive without the newest video game or high fashion clothing? Chances are they will survive just fine. What is more important is that they will be encouraged to re-evaluate the true meaning of Christmas, the celebration of the greatest gift of all, Jesus.

Jesus gave his heart to those he met while here on this earth. He touched people with love and compassion. As we celebrate his birth may we reflect that love and compassion to one another by sharing gifts of our heart rather than scurrying around frantically looking for an expensive gift at the top of a wish list in order to impress or pacify the receiver.

Now of course not everyone is able to appreciate gifts of the heart and some people may complain that it was a horrible Christmas arguing that they did not get one thing they wanted. What we want and what we truly need are often two different things. How often I hear people say if only I could have had one more day with, a letter from, or more memories with a person they loved.

Gifts are fun to get and they are fun to give. We like to see the surprise on our loved ones faces when we give them something they enjoy or feel the tingle of receiving a special gift. The gift however, does not have to require a lot of money or come from a long Christmas wish list. It is more valuable when it comes from the heart. Gifts of the heart can be created by our hands, our head or with our time.

The person receiving a heart gift will long remember the gift because it has lasting value. Material gifts (if kept and not returned!) can easily be replaced. God gave us the greatest gift of all, Jesus; let us celebrate Jesus' life by sharing our greatest gift with others, our heart. May God bless you every Christmas season and may you enjoy creating heart gifts for those you love.

Questions to ponder:
What is the greatest heart gift I ever received?
What is the greatest heart gift I ever gave?
How does giving and receiving heart gifts make me feel?

You Will Grow Into It

For whoever finds me finds life and receives favor from the Lord. —PROVERBS 8:35

It was a beautiful wintry morning and I was in need of focusing in on a topic. I had a number of ideas, titles and themes running through my head and was experiencing some difficulty deciding on a topic. It occurred to me that as I prepared to write this reflection that my spirit has been growing over the years and therefore my head is filled with all I have learned and all I want to learn. The topic then will be, growing into your spirituality.

My grandmother used to make clothing for me as a little girl for Christmas, and as I would open the gift she would always say to my mother, "I made it a little big so she can grow into it". I also recall receiving games as gifts, which were often for the next age group so that we could "grow into it". These are precious gems of wisdom today. I am stilling growing. My body may have stopped growing, but my spirituality is only beginning to grow and I am hoping I will grow into it!

My spirituality continues to grow as I continue to learn things about life. As I look forward to another holiday season I am reminded of many things I have learned to this point. Life is precious. Life is uncertain. Life is filled with joys and sorrows. This life is not fair. Wisdom is acquired over time. The people we love the most often receive our worst side. The little things in life are the most rewarding. Health should never be taken for granted. The simple things in life are the most beautiful. More is not better. The young are full of energy. Faith is hard at times. Life should not be rushed (I know many other tidbits of wisdom too numerous to enter in this writing!). And even as I have learned these truths, I continue to know them at a different level with each passing experience, with each passing day.

How can this reflection offer you any insight? Well, I am offering it to you with a request, an assignment of sorts. The month of December is always filled with lists of things you need to do, should do, or think you should do. Before you do anything stop and think about what you have learned in your life. Where do your joys come from? What makes life beautiful to you? Where does your comfort come from? What does money buy? What things cannot be bought? What do you celebrate?

I believe you will be surprised if you are truly honest with yourself, if you allow your spirit to reveal its growth. If you glean wisdom from your own spiritual growth perhaps you will find as I did that the most valuable things in life are free. Often the challenge is not just to know that the most valuable things in life are free, but then to give them freely without second guessing their value.

For example, consider the response of a friend, neighbor or family member when you bring them a plate of Christmas cookies? My experience has been one of gratitude in the expression of love offered through the generous gift of time evident on the plate. If you consider for a moment the dollar value of sugar cookies you will find that the ingredients for sugar cookies are not costly (unless of course you put elaborate sprinkles on top). You will also discover that the ingredients for these cookies are likely to be found in your cupboards at any given time. You do not need to run out and buy special ingredients. The most important ingredient for Christmas cookies is you. You are the maker, baker, artist and that is what shows up on the plate. Simple Christmas sugar cookies continue to be a welcome gift year after year because the value of love never diminishes.

As you prepare for the celebration of Christmas consider your inner wisdom before you run off to buy the perfect Christmas gift. I would venture to say that you have the perfect Christmas gift in your home already. You! Your uniqueness, talents, abilities, insights offer a multitude of gift giving ideas that will be far more valuable than anything you can buy with money.

Growing into your spirit, allowing yourself to use the wisdom from within will also alleviate some of the societal pressure around the holidays. It requires finding value in the gift that you are to others. Stepping out of the race takes courage. It is a sign however that you are growing into your spirituality. May God bless you and your families this Christmas with the gifts of spiritual wisdom found deep within.

Questions to ponder:
What does my spirit want to share?
How can I share my gifts with others?

A Season of Reflection

৶৶

Today in the town of David a Savior has been born to
you; he is Christ the Lord. —LUKE 2:11

৶৶

December! Many words come to mind for describing December. Cold, snow, Christmas, gifts, baking, parties, family and friends, worry, rushing, busy, spending money, frenzy, gratitude and peace are all words that one might use in describing the month of December. This reflection letter, however, is going to reflect on the word reflection. After all that is what the title suggests, but deeper, spiritual reflection.

Now I know in December you do not have a lot of time to be sitting around reflecting, there are after all, gifts to be purchased, decorations to be hung and cookies to be baked, but I would like to ask each of you to add just one activity to your December routine. Take some time for spiritual reflection. Christ lives in each person we meet, what does Christ look like in you? What to others see when they look at your face? Do they see the light of Christ in your eyes?

I can bet that each of you takes a look in the mirror after you wake from a deep sleep and I am stepping out on a limb here, shakes their head with surprise at how disheveled the night's sleep as made you look. Your hair is the classic "bed head" (a benefit for those with little hair, no "bed head"), there are wrinkles on your face "sleep lines", and "bags" under your eyes. But, look beyond your outer shell, deep inside lives the Holy Spirit, the light of Christ. December and the Christmas season give us an opportunity to check in and see how brightly the light of Christ is shining through our faces.

I want to suggest an activity for you to do during the Christmas season, one that will help you see the light of Christ in yourself and in others. I want you to add a new decoration somewhere in your home ideally the kitchen or dining room table. Place a hand mirror and a candle that you can pick up when it is lit, one with a handle would work well, on the table or another place you have chosen. Each day take the mirror in one hand and the lit candle in the other holding it so that it shimmers in the mirror. Then peer into the mirror at yourself. See the reflection of your face and the flicker of the candlelight. See the light of Christ within.

As you peer into the mirror ask yourself these questions:

1. How do I mirror Christ's love to others?
2. How have I reached out to others in need?
3. How do I show gratitude?
4. What am I being called to do in the name of Christ Jesus?

Initially, I suggest you do not use the bathroom mirror because it is often the reflection we criticize and the place at which we are most often rushed and quite possibly competing to use with other members of the family. Certainly, this space can grow to be a place where you can readily see the light of Christ and my hope is that it will, but for this activity please use it as a visible unusual Christmas decoration that might be shared with others who enter your home during the Christmas season.

I created a mantra for myself a few years ago and I sing it in the morning or whenever I feel the need to draw strength for the tasks of my day. The words are:

> Oh, Lord, my God I lift up my voice to you
>
> Oh, Lord, my God I offer my life to you
>
> Oh, Lord, use my life to mirror you
>
> May I be witness to those who seek you

I repeat these words over and over as I long to be more like Jesus. Though I fail many times I know I can call on God's strength to start again and re-ignite the light of Christ that lives in me.

It becomes all too easy to be caught up in the materialism of this world, but when we reflect on the true meaning of the birth of Jesus we remember God's love for each of us and the example God sent to be with us on this earth. Jesus mirrored God's love for each of us and we are called to continue the greatest tradition of all time, to reflect God's love to others. The spirit of God lives within each of us and in the Christmas season of reflection it should be fully kindled so as to warm the hearts of those we meet. May each of you be blessed with the reflection of Christ's' love in your mirror.

Questions to ponder:
Where can I place a hand mirror and candle?
How do I reflect God's love to others?
Who can I share God's love with?

Pay Attention

ᘰᘲ

Every good and perfect gift is from above, coming down from the Father of the heavenly lights, who does not change like shifting shadows. JAMES 1:17

ᘰᘲ

A New Year has begun and with the New Year we generally make all sorts of resolutions. We decide we will make big changes in our lives. Statistically, the majority of new changes fall by the wayside after a few months. I am going to suggest that you make one simple resolution and from this one resolution I believe you will be lead to a healthier lifestyle. Pay attention, that's it. Pay Attention!

I love the way these messages come to me and enjoy sharing them with you. I was walking one morning and felt a nagging irritation in the heel of my left foot. I considered the possibility of my sock slipping down and quickly reached down to adjust it hardly missing a step. You see I had a tight schedule that morning. I continued on my walk and the irritation became more intense. The following thoughts went through my mind, what a terrible pair of shoes; I cannot believe they are falling apart so quickly, I have not had them all that long. Before long I was altering my step to accommodate the pain in my heel. I had decided that I was not wearing these shoes again and I began to alter my schedule in my mind to include shopping for a new pair of shoes as soon as possible. Walking shoes need to be comfortable and have good sturdy support and because I walk several times a week I knew I needed to replace them as soon as possible. I resolved to fix this problem promptly by buying a new pair of shoes. The nagging irritation became worse. By this time

I was half a mile from the onset of the irritation and even further from home. I wondered how I would make it home in this pair of shoes.

Pay attention. Pay attention. The words whispered in my ear. I stopped. Investigated the irritated heel and smiled. I relatively large stone had lodged itself miraculously into a very unlikely spot in the heel of my shoe. I took a deep breath; paused in my routine and redirected my thoughts to focus more on the way God wanted to lead my day. God had a different plan for my day than I did. His list was different than mine. I guess that sometimes it takes a persistent stone in my shoe to get my attention! Beyond that, I listened to what God was telling me and I believe he used this situation as a way for me to understand and help others understand how quietly irritations can move into our lives and how misunderstood they can be.

As I thought about how quickly I was going to replace my shoes, I could not help but realize that we often do the same thing with other aspects of life. When we have a headache, we take a headache medication. When we have an ulcer, we take an ulcer medication. We jump from problem to solution without considering what might be causing the problem.

What are the stones in your life? How many have slipped in without you knowing? How many problems have you sought treatment for without uncovering the source of the irritation? When we are on the treadmill of life that our society dictates we avoid details that might cause us to stumble, fall, or have to drop out of the race. Unfortunately, we find out often too late that the details could have prevented us from acquiring chronic pain, a chronic illness, a disability, or a broken relationship.

Pay attention to the details of life. Listen to your body. Your body is a great advocate for personal health. The body can send out red flags that can help you identify the need for a change in your diet, exercise, rest pattern or relationship. But if you simply treat these flags as nuisances, you will never *remove* the stone. The stone, the irritation will continue to be with you. You may spend a lot of money trying to eliminate the irritation, but until the stone is removed you are only covering up or avoiding the real problem and you never solve the problem. You simply alter your step.

After a period of time we become accustomed to the altered step and may even forget about the stone, but the body does not forget about the stone and continues to carry it. And no matter how it is carried it will continue to rub and wear on the tissue, the mind or the spirit. Soon a wound will open. The open wound offers opportunities for infection, more damage to the body, mind or spirit. Whether your *stone* is an allergy to food, a need for forgiveness, a miscommunication, a need for peace in your life, a need for activity, or a need for a job change, carrying the stone unknowingly will cause a larger wound. It must be identified and removed.

We read in Psalm 139:1-6, "O Lord, you have examined my heart and know everything about me. You know my every thought when far away. You chart the path ahead of me and tell me where to stop and rest. Every moment you know where I am. You know what I am going to say even before I say it, Lord. You both precede and follow me. You place your hand of blessing on my head. Such knowledge is too wonderful for me, too great for me to know!"

God will help you identify your stone. God will lead your way and prompt you to rest. He has a plan for your relationships. He has a plan for your life. His plan for you is unique. You do not have to keep pace with this fast paced, treadmill running society. You can stop, rest, and reflect on his direction. Pay Attention to the message, the path, the light, or the whisper that God is presenting to you. Your New Year's resolution to Pay Attention will have a powerful rippling effect on you, your family and your community.

Questions to ponder:
Am I aware of the little things that irritate my life?
How can I resolve to open my heart to what the little irritations might be trying to tell me?
Will I tune in to God's whisper in the New Year?

Making Ends Meet

ℒℒ

Surely I am with you always, to the very end of the age.
—MATTHEW 28:20

ℒℒ

As I am writing this letter the year is coming to an end. Christmas is fast approaching and the tax bill has arrived. Somehow this time of the year lends itself to questions about making ends meet. In this reflection, however, I want to address another meaning for "making ends meet" as it applies to our spiritual health.

This reflection was prompted by a visit I had with a woman recently. We had a casual conversation about what to do when you feel pulled in different directions. She was feeling stressed in her job. She was questioning whether she might be experiencing "burn-out". She shared with me her initial love for her work and went on to say that although she could not put a finger on what it was that was moving her away from her earlier sentiments, she knew that each day was a struggle to come to work. She is certainly not alone. Many people have these feelings and although they share the desire to try something different for a while, they quickly qualify their desire with the reality of financial need and what a risk it would be in the current economic crisis to leave their job and look for something else. It seems to me their spirits are crying out for balance.

One of the things I always ask people when they express stress related to their commitments is whether they have taken time away from their commitments. They often cannot imagine taking time away when they are so swamped. They think it would only add to their stress rather than relieve it. This kind of thinking causes us to lose our spiritual balance. When our life is on a horizontal spectrum this focused attention to the commitment end offsets the balance and begins to tip our lives upside down, yet we often view our lives on a linear spectrum. Work on one end, rest on the other. Commitments on one end, dreams on the other. The ends of the spectrum can seem miles apart and we struggle to find a middle ground, a place for balance.

What if instead of settling for a middle ground we connected those ends and created a circle. God's strength can grasp each end of the spectrum and pull them together allowing us to incorporate our work, our commitments, our rest and our dreams in a form providing stability. Rather than having our spirit pulled in one direction and then another it can become fluid flowing from one thing to the next without feeling as though the balance is going to be too heavily weighted on one end and upset our whole being.

When God holds us together and stands in the center of your life the spectrum is less scary. If we envision a more circular fashion for our life, the view of our life is enhanced. We do not lose sight of where we have been, yet from the center of our being we can also see the opportunities more clearly for meeting our commitments and achieving our dreams. We can see how dependent each life event is upon another in the circle of life.

How can we begin to form a circular spectrum with Christ's love holding the ends together so that no one area of our life gets more attention than the other? There are a number of strategies but I believe the first one requires us to get to know ourselves a little better. Ask yourself this question, who am I? This question then requires an answer much deeper than a list of personal data. Beyond your name, place of residency, job title, household roles, and community memberships is a spirit that desires to be known. There is only one you, only one me. If I don't know me, how can I begin to be me? If you do not know who you are beyond these descriptors, how can you be you?

So, get to know yourself. Not who you think you should be, but who you are. Ask yourself these questions,

1. What do I believe and why? (Be sure to answer the why with more than, I just do!)
2. Where do I find peace and comfort?
3. Where do I find support in times of struggle?
4. When do I rest? How do I rest?
5. What do I want to leave with the world?

One question will likely lead to others, I encourage you to answer them. This process will not happen quickly, nor is it to be done only once in a lifetime. You see if your life is circular you will naturally come upon these questions again and you will need to answer them again. Everything you experience in life changes who you are and so the answers may change as well.

God's strength will support your spiritual balance as you step off the scale into the circle of life firmly supported by God's love. He will always be there holding our lives, yours and mine, making ends meet.

Questions to ponder:
Where do the heaviest burdens come from?
How will I find balance in my life?
Am I willing to let God pull the ends of my life into a ring of balance?

Incentive

For physical training is of some value, but godliness has value for all things, holding promise for both the present life and the life to come. —1 TIMOTHY 4:8

January is a time of the year when we think about motivating ourselves to achieve new goals. However, the cold and dark of winter can leave us feeling unmotivated at times. We often begin to look for incentives for our actions. As I thought about this I began to wonder about the incentives that motivate us into action. I want to discuss the topic of incentives and reflect on the need for and usefulness of added incentives.

We can be encouraged or inspired by a number of incentives. The maintenance of one's good health is an excellent incentive for eating right, exercising and getting proper rest. Having a family dependent on your care is an excellent incentive for working hard to provide food and shelter for those you love. These are two examples of positive incentives for getting us up and out of bed every day. They leave us feeling good about ourselves at the end of the day.

However, I would venture to say that there are incentives that do not leave us feeling the same goodness at the end of the day and which are perhaps clouding our ability to even identify the value of this feeling. Consider the incentives dangling in front of us to serve others. Do we really need to be offered some sort of recognition or monetary gesture in order to offer our service or assistance? God asks us to help one another. He speaks of our reward being in heaven, not of this world. Yet incentives are everywhere. Public recognition, free gift cards, gas cards, or drawings for prizes are awarded when we sign up to donate our time or donate money. Are we really donating then? Are we really giving unselfishly to someone else?

If you were running a race would it be the prize money or the feeling you would get from achieving the goal that would be the greatest incentive for you to enter? Anytime I have watched a race, a marathon or a bike race I have witnessed great joy on the faces of every participant as they cross the line, every participant, not just the winners. Why can't we focus on the *feeling* that comes from doing something good/well? Must there always be some incentive attached to our actions? Can the words good job, job well done, be just as good as the prize money? I believe the answer is yes!

Have you ever experienced true selfless giving? There is such joy that comes from a smile when you surprise someone with a visit, sharing your gift of time. There is an overall good feeling in your gut that comes from leaving a larger than necessary tip. I have had this feeling and although I am guilty of not doing it enough, I feel as though this feeling is the true incentive that should always be the motivating factor of any act of kindness or giving. I like to describe it as a tickling of my spirit. It is a great incentive. My spirit smiles when I have participated in a selfless act. It likes it. It wants more of it.

So how do we prepare our hearts for the race of life? What incentives do we need to have dangling in front of us to pull ourselves out of bed during the cold, gray days of winter? How do we let go of the desire to receive something for our actions? I wish I had a good answer to these questions. Ultimately, each of us has to look at these questions and apply them to our own life situation. Surely there is a time and place to be honored for one's accomplishments, to be rewarded for a job well done, but the day to day journey through life should be sprinkled with acts of kindness and giving, which are not in response to the earthly end result. They should be offered from the goodness of the heart trusting in the promise before us of a reward in heaven.

Questions to ponder:
What incentives do I need to do good works, take care of my health, or help a neighbor?
Will I model the value of living life for God's purpose solely without need for added incentives?

Acknowledgements

Thank you to my supportive family in always encouraging me to grow as I am being called to grow. They have been such a blessing in my life. I am grateful for their presence in my life beyond explanation.

My friends have walked with me down many roads and they know my journey well. Without the gift of friendship my life would have a large hole. I am thankful for each of the individuals God has given me to journey with.

A special thank you to the members of my community for the support and encouragement they gave me in creating this book. I have received so much love, support, and prayer from the community and I am eternally grateful.

Thank you for reading the messages God has sent to me. I hope they have had a positive impact on your life.

May God Bless you